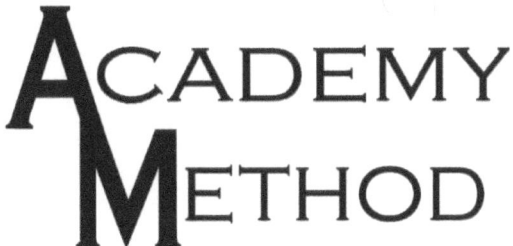

CADEMY
ETHOD

CLASSICAL BALLET
100 RULES

BY
KEN LUDDEN

A FONTEYN ACADEMY PRESS PUBLICATION

This book is intended as a textbook companion to the Academy Method Instructor Certification Program and should not be used for any other purpose. It was first published in this form to support the workshop series to develop choreography among promising students in Australia and New Zealand.

First published in hardcover by Lulu, December 20, 2017

ISBN: 978-1-387-45729-8

Printed in the United States of Americ

A FONTEYN ACADEMY PRESS PUBLICATION

TABLE OF CONTENTS

INTRODUCTION

This volume is for all dancers, even though it cites "ballet" in its title. By "ballet" we mean classical theatrical dancing in all its forms, and that this is being used as a fine art through which the dancer is able to clearly speak to the public.

However, there are many reasons for dancing, and many forms of dance. The basic rules and conventions set forth here allow any dancer, teacher, student or enthusiast to experience efficient movement, to avoid injury or unnecessary stresses to the body, and to have a harmonic organization of body in motion.

This volume includes two books: Book of Rules and Book of conventions. It is organized this way because the fine art form of classical theatrical dancing is sophisticated and refined. While the date for the organization into a schooling can be dated to 1671 in Paris, the art form began to develop in the 1500s as an activity at Royal Courts in Italy. When you date its inception is not considered in this volume other than to say that at the time of this first printing the history dates back more than 400 years in development. This is significant only in that it illuminates the fact that theatrical dance is rich in history, sophisticated in structure, and highly refined—so refined that it is indeed a Fine Art. As such, a dancer of concert performance is a fine artist, which means there is artistry in the decisions s/he makes while performing. The possibility of nuance, phrasing, dramatic expression, line, cadence, timing and position are available to the individual artist based on the precise control s/he has over every part of the body in motion.

To achieve that precision a dancer must know far more than the steps, and have teachers and coaches who have vast and personal knowledge. In these pages we expose this knowledge in two "books". First is the Book of 100 Rules, which give the student of the art form (a dancer learns throughout the entirety of his/her career, and even past retirement from the stage) insight as to why exercises are the way they are, and how to do them. Then, in the Book of 100 Conventions, the rich and diverse history is presented, with all of the recognized forms, traditions, and organizational elements that might be selected from among in performing choreography.

100 RULES

For many rules there are exceptions, and where there are exceptions, they will be listed beneath the rule. The listed exceptions are the main ones only. As dance is made up of choreographic languages that differ greatly from work to work, the dancer must find where exceptions may apply beyond those listed in this book. In the end, the goal is clear outward expression, so that any time a rule would inhibit that, then the circumstance would be a clear exception to the rule.

There are also some implications of rules, or ways they can be applied that may not be immediately apparent. In these cases, this will be discussed briefly beneath the rule in question. Dance has endless forms and uses. That said, a dancer must be intelligent and seek to find applications, implications and extensions of these rules as they progress through their dancing lives. Though the rules are given for ballet, they also apply to every form of dance, including forms not yet invented. Find the implications and then apply the rules liberally.

And finally, these rules impact each other, or work in tandem. Where there are specific interrelationships between rules, this will be indicated on the page that presents the rule. Dance requires coordination of the full body, and therefore a rule that applies to the legs, for example, will be related to a rule that applies to the arms or to a force of motion elsewhere in the body. Likewise, movement impacts the full body, and creates momentum that exists as its own independent element to be applied to the task at hand.

BOOK OF RULES

When Dame Margot Fonteyn said "teach what you know about dancing from having done it; no theories or philosophies, but only what you know from experience" she was reminding us all that dancing is an activity, not a philosophical discourse. Neither is ballet intellectual. And most decidedly it is a maximum achievement of what nature makes possible through the human being, and not a distorted and unnatural pursuit.

In this book the rules float above, around and outside of the technical specifics (Conventions) of the steps. There are basic principles of Newtonian physics that apply to all movement, and many of the rules in this book give the dancer instruction on how to approach them. Many of these are patterns of thought that when in the consciousness of the dancer cause the body to take maximum advantage of the laws of physics. Other rules have to do with the mechanics of the body, the organization of skill and the way to proceed most efficiently.

By following these rules an dancer is far less prone to have injuries, is far more in control of their body, uses energy efficiently and therefore can dance for more years because the wear on the body is minimized, and also has energy available for the full job of the dance, beyond just doing the steps. And because these are rules, they must be applied. They are not regulations to be followed or obeyed. Each rule, when remembered, experimented with, and then judiciously applied by the dancer is an opportunity to improve technique, and truly make artistic decisions.

SECTION 1. RULES FOR BALLET

Classical theatrical dancing, a centuries-old tradition, was borne as a concept in the Royal Courts of Italy in the late 1500s, but became codified system until 1671 in France under order of King Louis XIV. As such there are many traditions to the system, standards that both reflect the Royal origins and have proved to be the best way to assure its stature as a fine art form of highest human achievement.

This section "Rules for Ballet" is so named because these rules all have come from the study, practice and performance of classical dance. Indeed, these rules apply to any sort of serious study, practice and performance of dance, but in this publication the reference to origin is meant to respect the tradition, and certainly not to exclude any other form of dance.

By following these rules, dancers of any level (from beginning student to reigning Ballerina Assoluta) are able to achieve their highest and best potential, and perpetually continue to grow as artists. These rules are posted in the studios of The Margot Fonteyn Academy of Ballet, as a constant reminder for all who walk through our studios. They are also heard coming from the mouths of artists, faculty, and technical staff in classes and rehearsals, back stage, in dressing rooms and greenrooms, and whispered from artist to artist onstage during performances as constant reminders of the overall purpose – to achieve the highest expression of fine art possible – to which we are all dedicated.

THE MUSIC IS NEVER WRONG.

This is true without exception, even when a work or passage is danced in silence. For in ballet there is always rhythm, phrase, pattern and cadence.

Like in quantum mechanics, in which there is no time and place, and therefore no sequence, everything is first as it occurs. So, too, is this the first rule, even the other rules are all its equal. Breath, heartbeat, footstep, eurythmic pattern and the intuitive syncopation of life are always present in ballet, making it universal.

What is not wrong, is Truth. Music, for dance, is its truth.

DERIVATIONS:

► The tempo of the music must be fully accepted the moment it is heard;

► Pay attention to the mood and atmosphere the music brings, and respond to it;

► With live music, the musician is interpreting just as the dancer is, feel the nuances in dynamic, phrasing and expressiveness—match them;

► With live music, should there be an argument with the conductor or musician, save it for back stage, or some other area private from audience view;

► Learn everything you can about the music you dance to.

EXCEPTIONS:

► None.

THE STEP IS NEVER WRONG.

Dancing is ultimately about the choreography. Dance is an interpretive art form. As such, one never does an academic, classroom step on stage. So, in class or rehearsal, any step given is the step that must be mastered.

In addition, ballet is a fine art as is nearly all concert dancing. Fine art is refined, and so one must not just do the basic step given, but the precise step with nuances and embellishments, timing, internal rhythms, etc.

DERIVATIONS:

- ► Do not change a step to suit yourself or your ability; work on it until you can do it;
- ► Do not argue with the teacher or choreographer about what they have given you;
- ► Do whatever is necessary to achieve the step by the time of performance, or withdraw from the performance

EXCEPTIONS:

- ► The sentiment "the show must go on" applies here, for when in a performance situation there are always small inconsistencies and as a result there are sometimes when a step must be altered or adjusted so that the performance can continue. In such a case the idea of "choreographic intent" comes into play, for the artist must give the choreographic statement to the public, even if every detail of the choreography cannot be done.
- ► Over time choreography evolves, and with older works that can be extreme. Each artist brings their authenticity to each performance of a role, and this expands the interpretations, and sometimes raises the bar for certain steps. When such a work is restaged, the version of it being taught becomes the "authentic" one, while an artist is always encouraged to do in-depth study of the historic evolution of a role and then bring the very highest level they can to that role.

DANCE IS EXPRESSION, EVEN WHEN ABSTRACT.

Classical theatrical dancing is a fine art, and it is theater. Even abstract works are expressing their reality to the public. When required to play a character, it is clear how to determine the expression. But when playing a concept (the Miseries in *Giselle*, the various Temperaments in *Four Temperaments*, Fate in Choo San Goh's *Romeo and Juliet*, the Seasons in Ashton's *Cinderella*, ocean elements in Humphrey's *Water Study*, etc.) it is the job of the dancer to portray that concept clearly.

DERIVATIONS:

► Nureyev pointed out that every time a male dancer steps onto the stage he is representing the male gender as a whole, and it doesn't matter at all what one's sexuality, or opinion is—the expression of just standing there represents "male". This carries over to women, children and elderly people as well;

► One is always "dancing" so long as one is on stage or in the area of the dance, so even when there is no choreography given, one is sitting, or is just walking from place to place on the stage, the manner of stance, posture and locomotion must be done so as to express the proper element to the scene;

► Fonteyn points out that when playing an iconic character, it is important to incorporate the essential elements that character represents in each phrase of movement, rather than creating a detailed caricature of one's idea of that character's personage. This way every person in the public can see the personage they imagine, rather than finding the specifics at odds with their expectation.

► Even expressing noting is expressing something.

EXCEPTIONS:

► None.

EVERY CORRECTION IS A CORRECTION FOR YOU

Classical theatrical dance is a folk-art form; it is passed down from generation to generation. It has evolved from the early courts of Europe, and therefore has many unwritten rules, traditions and requirements of etiquette. It is also a fine art form, and requires absolute refinement and control over the body. Beginning as a child, as one must, the refined details are passed down constantly, and the conscientious student must be very aware in order to pick up the maximum information.

Teachers differ and their own bodies of experience of dancing are unique. Therefore, every word a teacher speaks is filled with their collective experience. The same is true of every choreographer, director, dancer, and related professional. Listen, listen, listen. And take every single word you hear as a personal opportunity for you to grow.

DERIVATIONS:

▶ Learn every role in every ballet you have access to;
▶ The only bad question is the one not asked;
▶ Keep a diary of class, rehearsal and performance notes;
▶ Watch every dancer and listen to what they are told, and see if and how they incorporate the correction into their dancing, as well as what impact it has;
▶ Never need to be corrected twice;
▶ Hang out in the studio to the maximum of your ability.

EXCEPTIONS:

▶ None.

TAKE CLASS NO MATTER WHAT.

To be a professional dancer has a minimum set of requirements. The body must be in a kind of top shape beyond all sports, for the movements and actions of the body are only a quarter of the mandatory elements that go into the mere perfunctory execution of steps. Yet the ability to dance properly stands apart from the other three: music, drama and sense of visual presentation to the public.

In order to place a movement precisely on a beat of the music; coordinate the trajectory of one body in purposeful relation with all other visual elements on stage; determine the exact speed at which one travels; place the body in motion (turning, jumping or traveling) in a carefully timed trajectory; and create an intricate pacing of expression for dramatic timing, the dancer must have absolute control over his/her body and every single muscle within it.

This takes a precision of movement that only comes from daily class six days per week without pause. And these classes must be classes that perfect, tune and further cause each dancer to grow and improve. To deviate from this has dire consequences, for a very short break from daily class results in a long period of hard work to return to the level prior to the break, and then at that point begin again to expand the technique and artistry of the body.

DERIVATIONS:

► 1 day off = 1 week to compensate; 1 week off = 1 month to compensate; 1 month off = 1 year to compensate

EXCEPTIONS:

► Dancers must take one day in seven off;
► After a tour or an extensive period of performing, dancers must take time off, but never more than two weeks in a row, and only then when there are at least two months of rehearsal period before the next scheduled performance;
► When a dancer or student is ill, it is imperative to do whatever is called for to return to health;
► Injured dancers must ease the way back into top shape.

WHEN YOU DANCE, DANCE FULL OUT.

"Performance begets performance." This is a phrase Dame Margot Fonteyn often spoke. Even in rehearsal one should do every step to its maximum and in the context of the character being played.

In class, when there is no specific character being played, the dancer must still execute each step with maximum expression, every time it is done. This trains the entire body to give itself to the dancing as a matter of course. Only this approach will produce a fine artist of dance; anything less will perhaps create a technician, but never an artist.

DERIVATIONS:

► When given a step, receive it in the context of the surrounding steps in the passage, this will allow you to know what the step is meant to be part of;

► Always ask questions, at the appropriate time, about each new step as to its uses, origin and significance—the more a dancer knows, the more a dancer shows;

► Study the origin of steps, history of usage of that step, and different choreographic settings in which a step has been used so that dancing it becomes 'informed' rather than rote;

► Watch other dancers doing the same step (in classes, on stage, in films, etc.) so that the full expressiveness of it can be imagined if not known;

EXCEPTIONS:

► There are classes and rehearsals that are immediately followed by exhausting performances, in which case to do a step as fully as possible while still reserving energy to properly give one's all to the coming performance;

► Doing the proximity of a step, or "marking" the step, is acceptable in many settings – for example when floor patterns are being worked out, or basic movement flow is being explored;

► When marking steps, always do the arms and upper body as fully as possible, including expression with face and body of the character, so that energy is reserved but the coming dancing is not sabotaged by bad habit.

DANCE EACH STEP AS IF IT IS THE LAST TIME YOU WILL EVER DO IT.

One must perform steps with absolute dedication to the effort. Whatever the state of your inner being, the audience will detect it. They will not know the details, but they will surely feel the essence of that feeling. Being tired, nervous, fearful or warry makes the audience feel similarly about your dancing, and about the expression being attempted. Being joyful, determined, confident and at ease will also be experienced by the audience and applied to what you are doing.

Trepidation, caution and hesitation represent the antithesis of theatrical dance. Audiences of classical fine art in all its forms want only two things: authenticity and integrity. When taking the stage in a classical dance, one must be fully committed, and completely empowered. It is impossible to achieve this by half measures. And so each time any step is performed, it must be an outward expression of an absolute inner commitment.

This is also true in class, and choreographic rehearsals. Grasping the steps performed in the same way that the drowning grasp a life preserver produces an entirely different sort of movement, expression and connection. Additionally, such an approach to movement makes one able to do miraculous things that can only be done with complete abandon and commitment. This is how to approach dancing.

DERIVATIONS:

- ▶ Whatever is going on inside of your heart and head will be read by the public;
- ▶ Having an internal action plan, or dialog, makes the audience relax and trust your performance as meaningful;
- ▶ Freedom from worries is freedom of expression;
- ▶ In dance, each moment is gone as soon as it passes without remnant;
- ▶ Giving yourself fully to each movement allows the body to use its full capacity without the inhibition of a thought process.

EXCEPTIONS:

- ▶ None

MOVEMENT CANNOT LIE.

It is impossible for the human to completely mask how one feels from one's movement, regardless the precision of one's training, or the intent to misrepresent one's self. In card games it is called one's 'tell'—those automatic kinetic impulses that occur when one is excited, disappointed, confused, hesitant, etc.

Beyond those micro-responses in the body, there is meaning in basic movements. When one is reaching for something, the fact is they want that thing. It is undeniable truth. When one turns one's back on someone, they do not wish to remain involved. There are hundreds of basic movements people do that, by virtue of the fact one is doing that movement indicates intent, which reflects feeling.

DERIVATIONS:

►   What one does not do speaks as truthfully as what one does do;
►   Cunning and dishonesty show through movement;
►   Sincerity shows through movement.

EXCEPTIONS:

►   Illness of any kind (physical, emotional, psychological, mental, etc.) may render movement independent of truth.

HOW YOU FEEL, THE AUDIENCE FEELS.

People relate to people. Watching children play makes people smile. Witnessing an argument makes people uncomfortable. Watching a fight makes people concerned, afraid and sometimes angry. It is only possible to override the instinct to relate through rigorous training (e.g., military or martial arts training, medical training, clinical training, etc.).

In addition to the fact that people relate to one another, intuition is also at play. When someone is uneasy, others sense this. The same is true with inner states such as frustration, intrigue, anticipation, attraction, and many more. The fact is that what one feels is picked up to some extent by those watching.

A theater audience has come specifically for the purpose of empathetic or sympathetic viewing. The audience will even suspend their basic belief in reality just to get the most out of their experience. Choreographers, librettists, playwrights, directors and other theater professionals base their designs on this. And in a ballet audience, people expect to be thrilled, and dismayed by the amazing and super-human things being done before them.

DERIVATIONS:

► Create a story in your mind when you dance that gives your movements meaning and motivation;
► Leave your day to day concerns outside of the studio or theater;
► Experience the actual feelings indicated by the choreography as you perform the role;
► Intentionally create the emotional journey for your audience when you dance.

EXCEPTIONS:

► None.

A DANCER GIVES TO THE ROLE; THE ROLE DOES NOT GIVE TO YOU.

Building a career of note only happens when each time you take the stage you add something to the role you are dancing. You have been entrusted to speak the choreography to the public in your authentic voice, interpreting it anew with each performance, building depth and breadth to the choreographers' statements. As with singing, you must stand behind the material you are presenting, allowing the work to be alive through you.

Those who place their own ego in front of the work, who take a new role as an opportunity to promote themselves add nothing to the art form. This approach builds a resume rather than a career. Ballet has a long history, and to take your place as part of that living history in your own time will only happen when you use your artistry to add to the role.

DERIVATIONS:

► Study the history of every ballet you do to learn everything that has been done already;

► Study other artists in the same role and find the thing not yet said through it, that is authentic for you as an artist and human being;

► When a role is created on you by a choreographer, delve deeply into the statement being made and bring your authentic truth into that statement;

► Be ever humble to the profound history of classical theatrical dance;

► The 40th performance of a role by the same artist is the first truly authentic interpretation of that role by that artist.

EXCEPTIONS:

► When being coached in a role by an authoritative voice, temper your own interpretation—at first—to what is being taught to you to do with it.

THOUGH ANOTHER MAY BE 'BETTER'; YOU WERE ASKED—SO DO IT.

Each artist is unique; there can be no competition between interpretations of a role. As an artist you must stand in absolute confidence of yourself and your own artistic instincts. Dancers, and some others within the dance world, often think that technique is all that matters, and therefore the one who can perform the steps the best is 'better' at dancing. This approach trivializes the fine art into a superficial, vapid display of mechanics of body.

Ballet is not circus, nor is it commercial entertainment, it is a fine art form. There are many, many reasons a dancer is given a role to dance. Do not waste energy worrying about your insecurities—just give yourself fully to each role you are given to dance.

DERIVATIONS:

- ► Be confident and trust your directors in their choices;
- ► Pay attention to your dancing only, there can be no comparison between artists;
- ► Fulfill each moment you dance, give it your very best; there is nothing more you can give;
- ► Most criticisms of comparison are derived from jealousy rather than a true assessment.

EXCEPTIONS:

- ► None.

MUSIC IS BETWEEN THE NOTES; DANCING IS BETWEEN THE STEPS.

It is quite easy for teachers, students, choreographers and professional dancers alike to pay so much attention to technical details that the actual flow of dancing ceases to exist. In these cases the movement becomes mechanical, flat and dull. But dancing is expression, and so it is up to the dancer to dance the choreography, not just do the steps. A ballet makes a visual, kinetic statement in all cases, and it is also expressive. This combination of statement and expression is why the art form exists.

DERIVATIONS:

- ► If one is taking part in a dance, even when standing in line to the side or moving into position to begin a sequence, every single transition from one movement to the next must be artistically presented;
- ► Rehearse all transitions;
- ► Create a world that is complete;
- ► Choreography ought never be presented as classroom steps, there is always a sense of it that is unique to that phrase or ballet;
- ► Dancing happens in phrases—phrases are united.

EXCEPTIONS:

- ► None.

FORWARD IS YOUR FRIEND.

The way the body is built, it assumes forward movement. The fact that the toes of the foot are in front, and when turned out the strongest toe is in the front, means that a forward inclination of the body is where the balance point is whenever a body moves. This is further represented with the system of arms in ballet and dance, which are usually slightly in front of the body.

A dancing posture₁ is one in which the vertical axis of the body is forward approximately 5°; a resting posture is when the vertical axis of the body is upright. Therefore, except for Combré, all ballet positions utilize this forward tilted stance as point of origin. This assumes that the weight of the head (the human adult head weighs on average between 10 and 14 pounds) is aligned on top of the spine without a forward drop or backward tilt. It also assumes that the psoas is engaged so that the entire body from toes to hair is in a unified and coordinated upright stance.

DERIVATIONS:

▶ If you are looking down with the head and eyes, some part of the body is displaced behind the central balance line;
▶ A true balance will feel at first as if you are about to fall forward;
▶ Use your arms.

EXCEPTIONS:

▶ Combré;
▶ Counterbalance between two bodies;
▶ Partnering.

---

1 In olden days, stages were raked (meaning they were tilted downward toward the public at an angle between 8° and 14°). This required the dancers to pull back the upper-most torso so that the dancer would not fall forward as they moved or stood on the stage. This backward angling of the shoulder blades, neck, head and upper-most torso gives a look of pride and importance when done on a flat stage. In the 20th Century construction techniques for theaters changed so that the stage is flat and the audience is raked. And until the late-1960s most opera house stages were still raked. But beginning in the 1970s there was a fundamental shift in new construction of theaters, and it became more usual that dancers danced on flat stages.

IF YOU CAN'T DO IT FULLY, DON'T DO IT.

Dancing is one of the endeavors that only works when it is done fully. Diminishing a step (called 'marking' the step) changes the tempo, height, rhythm, distance, speed and expressiveness. To develop as a dancer, one must dance fully or you have wasted time and energy.

In addition, it takes 100,000 repetitions of a movement for the body to do it automatically, without thinking about it. When the movements have developed to this level, then the dancer can do the steps fully and at the same time can focus on phrasing, musicality, expressiveness, character development and other overall arcs that occur when performing. If a movement is done in a half-measured way, then that way of doing the step is establishing itself on the road to becoming automatic. And so to progress to the maximum, doing the step fully every time you do it gets you there faster.

When planning how much space or time it takes to dance a sequence, the only way to reliably know is for it to be done fully. And when there are series of movements designed to align with music in specific ways, the only useful way of trying to do it is to do it fully.

DERIVATIONS:

► Give yourself completely to your dancing;
► The easier, softer way is to do it full out every time;
► One only grows as a dancer by dancing every time as fully as possible.

EXCEPTIONS:

► In rehearsals it is sometimes helpful to mark a step to refresh the memory, or to have the music become fully integrated into one's focus;
► When a step is first given by a teacher or choreographer, marking it to get the basic sequence is helpful;
► When new to a dance with little time to learn it just prior to a performance, marking through it with the others in that section helps bring it into focus and active physical memory.

CLASS IS TRAINING; WARM-UP IS PREPARATION FOR CLASS.

Building a fine art career requires constant growth, refining technique, and economizing movement and energy. Fine art careers excel by the ability to intentionally shape a unique expression. Dancing is a fine art form. And daily class lays the foundation for that day's activities.

In addition to the insistence that daily class is for training rather than warming up the body, the structure of a training class is such that it prepares the dancer for the type of endurance and flexibility required on stage. And when choreographers are creating or rehearsing their works, they must be able to see the dancers grow within the kinetic language of that particular piece.

Dancers, as fine artists of the concert stage, build a career. Commercial dancers will simply fill their bookings calendar with 'gigs' to ensure earnings, but do not build a career as an artist. To achieve a career, and to be competitive with the great accomplishments in classical theatrical dancing from the late 1500s to the present day, a dancer must have a full class 6 days per week.

DERIVATIONS:

▶ Your approach to your morning class sets the dynamic for that entire day of dancing;

▶ The only time there is nothing more to learn is after one retires from the field of dance, not only from active dancing;

▶ Slacking off in class leads to injuries;

▶ A fine art form is dead when it rests on the status quo.

EXCEPTIONS:

▶ When there is a double performance day, it is appropriate to do a training class at the start of the day, and a warmup before the second performance;

▶ Upon returning from an injury or an extended time off from dancing, one's approach to the first few classes is best to be simply as preparing the body without requiring full training, but only during the first half of the first week back;

▶ In full production mode, each 7th consecutive daily class should be a warmup only.

SECTION 2 - BALLET PARADOXES

Life is filled with paradoxes – two things that appear opposite but are both true. Ballet is life, so ballet also has its paradoxes. In fact, ballet has 9 paradoxes. These 9 paradoxes are among the foundational and fundamental rules of ballet. And it is those to which this section is dedicated.

Ballet paradoxes serve as guides to all who participate in the fine art form. These paradoxes assist in making decisions about how and where to spend one's energy, including how to approach the decision process between tasks or methods of achieving goals.

For the dancer these paradoxes speak to how to spend and apply body energy; how to draw the line between physical capacity and artistic integrity; and how to reduce the stresses that encumber you. These paradoxes must be ingrained fully in the subconscious of the dancer so that they become instinctive. Once this has been achieved, it transforms that artist's performance evermore.

For the teacher these paradoxes direct how and what you correct; what to give in class; how to set the standard for achievement for each student; how much and how fully to dedicate yourself to teaching; and what to hold onto or let go of. If a teacher has had these ingrained in their dancing career years, then they will carry over automatically to the teaching. But they must be applied differently. As a dancer they are applied within the body and mind; as a teacher they are applied to the craft and how you integrate with it.

For a choreographer these paradoxes help make the basic structural decisions that become the framework of choreography. They guide how you speak to the dancers so they will become one with the choreography; how and when to make a statement; how much to assign to the sister arts of music, lighting, costume, etc.; and which statements are to be made and to whom. A choreographer must be freed from their own mundane life circumstances so they can speak across time; and yet be fully authentic and personally present even when the choreography is interpreted by many dancers over time.

For a director they help organize resource allotment, and how to make decisions that will be applied globally to one's own realm. They help the director to remain focused on the large picture while paying attention to details; how to wear the many hats the job requires, and how to switch between those different hats.

These paradoxes reach into every moment of the life of every artist and technician in this fine art field. By instilling them early into the dancing years, they will serve the dancer forever. And they will also apply to the life of the artist. Even as a young dance student, and ever after, the participant in ballet will have to be the ambassador for the art form and its demands on them. By using these paradoxes, that fine line of distinction can be maintained with greater ease.

LESS IS MORE.

Dancing is natural and entirely human. Theatrical dancing is highly organized, but relies on adequate repetition through rehearsal to become natural to the dancer. Adding that theatrical dancing is meant to express universal elements of the human condition, the more natural the movement, the more effective it becomes as an authentic expression. Any forced effort instantly transforms the expression from natural to contrived. When one does "more", one expresses less, therefore proving the paradox in terms of expression.

This paradox, however, goes far deeper than the expression. When a movement is automatic, it is both efficient and fluid. Allowing the muscles to do their work without relying on conscious thought for guidance, the myriad combinations of muscular activity is coordinated by the nervous system itself. This is far faster than conscious thought, and absolutely inclusive of the entire body. The conscious mind is limited on its ability to focus, and when relied upon as the driver of the body's movement will over focus on select elements and ignore the others. Somatic sense is natural to humans, and it includes a sort of trust in the natural and automatic functions of the body, while blending one's expressive and experiential continuum to guide and form overall arc without interfering with basic coordination. Any concentrated focus on one element of movement results in clumsy movement. To do less allows these brilliant senses of the body to do their maximum.

AWARENESS OF A THING EXISTS ALSO IN THE ABSENCE OF THAT THING.

Without silence there is no rhythm. In fact, the absence of sound is just as powerful in creating rhythm as the sounds that are heard. Beyond that one of the most powerful tools in music is the absence of something that is expected to be there. Likewise, the same is true in movement, speech, and all forms of expression. Comedic timing is more about silence than sound.

Likewise, in expressing a dramatic narrative through movement, the awareness of a character must remain throughout the work, even when the character is not on stage in a particular scene. In Romeo and Juliet it is essential that both characters be in the minds and hearts of the public at all times. It is the scenes in which one of the lovers is present and the other absent, that the absence has the most power presence.

UP IS DOWN.

Quite literally, to go up into the air is accomplished in large part by pushing down with the legs. In addition, the higher a part of the body is (an arm or a leg, for example) the more powerfully it falls when it comes down.

This paradox is also about contrast. The higher something is in elevation, the more pronounced the effect of the landing. An example of this is found in the *Giselle* Act II grand *pas de deux* between the characters Giselle and Albrecht. At opposite sides of the stage, both do a *sousous* with full 3rd *porte de bras* that leads into *chassé a côté, pas de bourré, glissade, assemblé éliogné*. The two dancers cross past each other, each beginning on the opposite side of the stage from where they end, accentuating the sense of polar diversity but also balance of opposites (a paradox in itself). But there is more. When in the air the leading arm is lifted high in an open high 5th position, and then on landing the arms, head and torso fall dramatically to the ground, and the leading hand brushes the floor as it joins the other arm coming to rest in a very low 5th position. The choreographic statement is about life after death and having left the earthly realm behind, and below. The higher the jump, and the greater fall to the floor, the more dramatic the effect.

RULE 19: PARADOX 4

UNDERSTATEMENT HAS MAXIMUM POWER.

For centuries those in power have used understatement to accentuate and proclaim their power. To be above reacting to things that would cause a normal person to have a strong reaction denotes a state of ease in face of calamity. This ease demonstrates that a person has protection, resource, assistance or some other strength that allows them to remain unbothered. This is a clear demonstration of power, shown through understatement.

Royalty uses this, as do powerful individuals in politics, military force, medical personnel, security forces, diplomatic corps, parenting and more. It is the hyper-reactive response that denotes vulnerability, insecurity and a sense of weakness. An advertising campaign for anti-perspirants uses the phrase "never let them see you sweat" as a way to demonstrate one's power in every situation.

In dancing, this takes on a slightly different meaning. When a dancer exaggerates every movement, the public cannot see the finesse and subtlety a truly powerful dancer can show. Seeing circus tricks is exciting, but showing refined technical prowess, and the use of this to make a statement really holds power in it, the power to impact the public.

Indeed, the greater the ability to use refinement in dancing, the more powerful the artist with the audience.

LESS EFFORT, FASTER MOVEMENT.

One of the many benefits of automatic movements that are the result of repetition in training is that the lack of conscious thought directing the body to move, the more efficiency there is in achieving the movement. This means that only the muscles involved in a movement are used, and then they are only used precisely as much or as little as necessary to accomplish the movement. Not only is there less (almost none at all) effort required to do a movement, there are also no conflicting muscles pulling against the movement.

One way to achieve this is for dancers to focus on phrasing rather than steps, and beyond that on overall expression. This expression may be a character, a mood, an element of music made visible through the steps or many other things. For example, in a *grand assemblé de volé*, by directing the dancer to focus on lifting the chest, leading with the top of the head, or the reach of the fingertips of the leading and lifting arm, no effort goes into the batterie, and that makes the beats quicker, cleaner and far more facile.

The same is true for long balances, or sustained turns as well. By diverting the applied effort away from the mechanics of the step, the dancer's body will simply fall into place and easily lift above the turn. In this case balance and maintaining a position are automatically crafted with ease by the body in a very natural way. There is no visible effort, no strain, and beautiful fluid movement.

YOU ARE NOT FREE UNTIL YOU DECIDE WHAT TO CONNECT YOURSELF TO.

This paradox was often said by Miss Craske[2] in class. When she used this, she was most often referring to dancers who were not free to commit to a step or danced phrase because they were torn between concerns like line, technique, character expression, musicality, phrasing or any of the many elements that make up the whole of dancing. By simply deciding which element the dancer was connecting with, the dancer is then free to simply do that thing to the utmost, nearly always having a spectacular and successful result.

There were many other times that this was used, however. IF a dancer is physically present in the studio, but mentally focused elsewhere, there is a conflict that makes it impossible to dance, and impossible to take care of the thing on one's mind. Again, by simply making the commitment to be fully present (connected with) what is happening in the studio, one becomes free to dance fully and effectively.

Dancers in modern society are often faced with subtle or quite forceful ridicule for choosing a life in the fine arts rather than going into a career that is more commercially viable. Many brilliant dancers, many whom may have been a leading icon of their generation, had lackluster careers because they were torn. Trying to dance while secretly believing there was a way to turn fine art into a commercial success, they were unable to connect to either of these mutually exclusive worlds. The same has been true for commitment to relationship or lifestyle.

Indeed, after decades of observation, this paradox cements itself as one of the most powerful truths of life, for until one decides what they are connected to, they are forever torn between possibilities, second guessing every choice they make, and maintaining chaotic inner turmoil. Until it is resolved, decision made, there is no freedom at all.

---

2 Margaret Craske (November 26, 1892—February 18, 1990) was a British ballet dancer, choreographer and teacher of ballet. Soloist in Les Grandes Ballets Russes, student of Enrico Cecchetti and designated by him and Anna Pavlova to be "the teacher" of her generation. Founder of the Metropolitan Opera Ballet, and teacher at Julliard. Author of: The Dance of Love: My Life with Meher Baba, , Theory and Practice of Advanced Allegro in Classical Ballet with F.Derra De Moroda

THE DEEPER YOU GO IN A PLIÈ THE MORE YOU LIFT THE TORSO.

This is the opposite of Paradox 3 "Up is Down". While technical in nature, through application it becomes far more central to the art of dancing. When landing from a jump, or preparing to ascend, the demi-plié is critical. When the heel is firmly planted on the ground, and the body weight is centered on the plantar surface of the supporting foot (or feet), the leg can contract to its maximum and the dancer maintains control and power. The act of consciously lifting the torso when dropping to the depth of a demi-plié the hips remained lifted with psoas engaged, and the body weight is lifted away from the knees and ankles. In turn, without feeling the full weight of the body drop onto these overused and often fatigued joints, they will relax and remain pliable.

However, if the full weight of the torso lands heavily on the hips and transfers to the knees and ankles, these joints react by tensing up. The ball of the foot pushes against the floor in a reflex action which means the Achilles tendon is engaged, thus placing strain on it. The knees will be pulled out of alignment of the many leg muscles that seek to protect them, thus straining the ligaments. And the quadriceps engage, making it nearly impossible for the hip joints to bend, as they attach on the top above those joints. This will ultimately result in a series of injuries, and greatly shortens the lifespan of the dancer's career.

THE STRONGER THE MUSCLES, THE LESS FLEXIBLE THE JOINT.

Many dancers pine after the hyper flexible knees and ankles of those with a natural tendency to flexibility. The line of the extended leg and foot of such dancers is beautiful to behold, and is often held up as an aesthetic ideal. Many lesser informed teachers will even call such a natural flexibility "talent". The plight of such dancers is a constant fear of the weakness of their joints, and many of them will drop out of dancing when faced with advanced pointe work, or rigorous dancing. Their joints are simply too weak to sustain the endurance required of a professional dancer.

On the other side of the fence, those flexible and weak dancers look with wonder and envy at the ones who are solidly built, strong, and able to jump, balance and turn without risk of injury at every attempt. The body lines of such dancers is not so spectacular, but is still quite beautiful. All the while, these dancers stretch and stretch and stretch and stretch, finding themselves ill-suited to a life of dance because their photographs do not look like the extremely flexible. They often lament that they are called to stand in when the flexible ones sustain injuries, and no matter how hard they are pushed, they rarely falter. They sometimes feel doomed to a life of being second cast but having to be on call to stand in at all times.

The fact is, the more muscle, tendon, ligament and bone strength, the less flexible the joints, the less elastic the muscles. Regardless of which side of this divide your natural body is, the WAY you work will balance it. Trying to be something you are not cannot be successful. Best to know where your strengths and flexibilities are, and work with them.

Take Class and Stretch Daily; If You Cannot Dance Full Out, Do Not Dance.

Yes, dancers must take class 6 days per week no matter what. Without this daily exercise, with one day of rest, the body deteriorates from its readiness to tackle the fine art of theatrical dancing. On the other hand, a half-measure attempt will instantly establish itself as the norm, and immediately begin to take away from your ability to do what is required. And so, if you cannot do the class, step, or rehearsal full out, it is actually damaging to your dancing to do less than the most.

So how does this work? How does one make the call on a day when there is something inhibiting the ability to do it completely, full out? This is the most challenging of the 9 paradoxes of dance. It means that every moment a dancer is dancing, they must be doing their best. At the same time, perpetrating an injury, or even risking one, is a very bad thing to do. And so at every moment a dancer must make critical choices.

At the Academy there is a basic rule we teach students: if you are working your body it will likely hurt. Every athlete knows that working the muscles can make them sore. But, when what is being done or attempted is hurting you, causing injury, then stop immediately. The difference is very great, though it sounds quite similar—something hurting is different from something hurting you.

SECTION 3 - ETIQUETTE RULES

Ballet originated first in the Venetian Court of Katherine di Medici in the late 1500s but did not become formalized until a century later in the courts of Louis XIV of France. It remained a courtly cultural form for another near century before it became a Royal offering to the public, and a means of communicating with them. Due to this there are many traditions and conventions that remain intact to this day. These are unwritten, until now, and mainly passed down through example rather than teaching. It is very difficult for a person who has not been introduced to this world and its etiquette as a child to understand it, though not impossible.

The nine rules of etiquette here are the central and universally upheld ones. They are the foundation upon which ballet has developed and been passed on, evolved and flourished, and also survived times of social unrest or political upheaval. Each studio, company, teacher, choreographer, dramaturg and ballet master will have his or her own specifics that are emphasized or required. The rules below are the basic rules of etiquette from which these specific cases evolve.

Learn these rules well, and understand that in each formal ballet setting they will be present in some form. Look for these and follow them. When a dancer observes the form and spirit of these rules, they earn the respect of the system itself, as reflected in the various individuals present.

It is by following these rules, holding the traditions in very high esteem, that one is ultimately granted the freedom to have full artistic range of expression available to them. And one is granted this freedom, it is not simply presumed or taken.

ACKNOWLEDGE TEACHERS, PIANISTS, STAFF AND ADMINISTRATORS.

Ballet is a folk fine art form, passed down from one generation to the next, mainly by example. You will find that your teachers, choreographers, and esteemed guest artists often tell stories of their encounters in the ballet world. They are not just being old and repeating themselves, even if it seems they are. These stories are the fables that carry the deep knowledge of the intricate system of etiquette and practice that has produces this high art form and kept it powerful for centuries. Listen to the stories, ask questions (particularly if something seems really strange) and consider the answers. It is in these fables that you will find great treasure, and ultimately develop a personal code of conduct that will carry you through your career.

These nine etiquette rules are just the base. They take many forms in studios and classrooms around the world. Take the first of these, Rule 25, for example. It simply means that one should acknowledge the others who work to bring you into the ballet world with knowledge, technique, opportunity and viability. But what, exactly, "acknowledge" means will change from one setting to the next.

For example, at the end of a ballet class there are all manner of etiquette conventions. The most common one is to applaud the teacher, who during this will indicate the accompanist (if there is live music). Many schools have each student curtsey or bow to the teacher, lining up single file before him or her as they exit the studio. Sometimes there is a phrase spoken by each student, or an exchange of some sort. Often in the professional world dancers just leave, and sometimes even during the class itself. Because of the great variance of this, and other such practices, it is not included specifically. Instead it is an extension of Rule 25.

Find out how acknowledgement of elders and teachers is done and then simply follow suit. This rule developed during the days of the Courts of Europe, and many of the Monarchs responded with terrible violence to any infraction. The Danish kings would exterminate anyone who imitated or mocked them. When a dancer placed his or her arms in high 5th position, the position of the arms called *"en corrone"* (meaning "crowned"), it was interpreted to mean that the artist was proclaiming that they were Monarch! This was high treason and had terrible results. And so the arms in Danish dancing are quite low, so they would never be misunderstood.

Likewise, one never addressed a Royal first, and never looked upon the Royal person unless specifically invited to. Since looking at the audience is the dancers' way of addressing those present, one would never turn the head so the face went to the audience. Instead, the head is inclined, but not turned. To do otherwise was an affront.

In today's world, the etiquette remains, but the consequences are much different. However, in a formal, classical ballet setting, to break etiquette can still have disastrous results for a dancer's reputation and future career.

EVERY PERSON DESERVES RESPECT; NOBODY IS SO MUCH BETTER THAN ANOTHER THEY SHOULD BE DISRESPECTED.

The ballet world is multi-layered with strict hierarchy. And this is true for every part of it, not only in the studio or on stage. It is also true in the dressing room, the board room, and in every technical department (wardrobe, props, shoes, etc.). Professional theater, more than any other workplace in the world, is the primary example of each person doing his or her job, yet being aware of and dedicated to the whole being accomplished.

The system works when there is a foundation of respect for all departments. Many head strong, egotistical dancers have learned that being insulting or demeaning to the conductor, the lighting designer, the costumer, etc., can have a very bad result. Each individual is just as important to the whole being accomplished as any other. Yes, the star gets the most attention and highest pay; yes, the director has the most power; etc. But dedication to the art form itself is the proper priority, not one's self.

And yet, in the performing arts there are many people with huge egos and huge insecurities who find they need to bully others with disrespect to elevate themselves. Some young dancers see this and think it is the way to be important, the way to be a big star. It is not.

One must adopt a code of personal conduct that is consistent regardless of what others do. This personal code is mostly established by age 7, but throughout life one can always improve and grow. The etiquette rules within the ballet world are such that one acknowledges the position of the other, but does so with respect. This respect demonstrates the appreciation for the role the other person plays, but reflects the basic foundation that all living things deserve respect regardless of their role.

THE MOMENT YOU KNOW YOU CAN'T DO A PROMISED TASK, ALERT THOSE WHO EXPECT YOU.

Nobody can do everything they have been assigned to do, or have signed up to do. Life just doesn't allow it, because life is dynamic and constantly changing. But everyone in the ballet world must take responsibility for what they have been assigned. And so, the moment something changes that will prevent fulfilling a promise there are two things to do. First, alert people. Let them know you will be late, or unable to do what is expected. Then, make every effort to replace yourself, so that the show can go on. And it is unusual that a change happens after the appointed time. So the moment of realization is well before anyone would miss you. They should never have to wait for you, not knowing where you are or what has happened.

For those who make a practice of this, there are several direct benefits. First, people will trust you, and they will know they can rely on you. Second, if you are in the habit of keeping people current, then should there be a situation in which you cannot alert them, they will not be angry but rather concerned. In addition, people will like to work with you, and they will like you. No matter how professional an encounter, it is still humans, and humans work better when they like each other.

A career is built as much on the stage as off. Having a good reputation, and being dutifully reliable in all things will give you a far richer career.

IN CLASS ONLY PAY ATTENTION TO YOUR OWN DANCING.

The dancer has a job: to dance. And the state of an art form is reflected in the integrity of each individual who participates in that art form. One must do one's best, and always seek to improve. It is impossible to do any of this if attention is given to others, and not kept firmly on the self. It does not mean to be selfish or self-absorbed. It means to be focused on your own work, your own dancing, your own flaws and your own strengths.

It takes 12 years from the first dance class to create a beginning professional dancer. It then takes another 10 years of constant dancing in a professional setting to truly become an artist. This means that if a child starts at age 6, they will be ready to enter a company around age 18, and be established as an artist by age 28. Then the real work begins, for once established as an artist, artistry must develop and grow.

The more focused a dancer is on his or her own dancing, the higher level they will achieve; the more a dancer is focused on other dancers or events in the studio, the lower the level they will achieve. And companies are always wanting to increase their prowess as an artistic tour de force. The dancers who are not developing, and who plateau at a low level of artistry or technique will ultimately be passed over for promotion, and eventually dropped from the roster. It is very simple.

ENTERING A STUDIO SAYS YOU WILL DO WHAT IS ASKED OF YOU.

The very act of crossing the threshold to studio (or stage) demonstrates a commitment to do one's very best. It shows intent to follow instructions given, without dissention, argument, refusal or emotional resistance.

It has been repeatedly stated that classical theatrical dance is a folk fine art form, passed down from one generation to the next by teaching, example and corrections. In each class and rehearsal one or more of the elders of the dance tribe is actively passing down the knowledge to keep the art form alive. It cannot be over-emphasized how important it is to listen, learn, try, absorb and be fully present.

Dance is also a living, evolving fine art form. There are innovators, visionaries and creators present. Innovation always comes in the form of breaking a rule, exploring a previously unexplored region, or going against an established grain. It will seem "wrong" often. As a dancer you must not resist. You are the clay in the sculptor's hands.

Your teachers in class are dedicated to improving your dancing to the highest level possible. This enables you to have the maximum control over your body so that you can deliver whatever the choreographer asks. Your rehearsal director, if coconscious, will tidy up your spacing and timing but more importantly direct your focus to the manner in which you interpret your expression. And so on. Each person gives you something essential, whether you think so or not.

Should the work being required of you by an individual is problematic in a serious way, the answer is to not cross the threshold into a studio they direct.

REMEMBER WHAT YOU HAVE LEARNED.

Anything taught, instruction given, choreography created, and/or individual correction is to be carried forward in all subsequent work on that aspect of dancing, as the sacred duty of the dancer. Top tier professional companies sometimes have a rule that if a dancer is given the same correction a second time, then they are fired. This is extreme, but it does exist. The fact is that each dancer must retain what they have learned from day to day. And if that takes hours of review at home, extra time in the studio before class, or outside help, so be it. It is the duty of the dancer to do what it takes to retain and expand on everything learned.

This is particularly true when new choreography is being created. It is expected that the dancer will not only retain what has been created, but will work on their own to assimilate it into their body. Once assimilated, the dancer can then proceed to develop their interpretation of the work. It cannot be ignored that choreography is expression in a dialog between the choreographer and the public. The dancer is its Ambassador, and must deliver it authentically, in their own voice, while being truly representative of the choreographer's intention—dancer is actor; steps are dialog.

To authentically deliver a choreographic expression with the integrity of one's one true voice is the ultimate reason for theatrical dance. This is impossible if the dancer does not know what is being expressed. Any time taken to relearn a passage keeps the dancer from discovering the fundamental expression and its nuances (often supplied by the dancer).

And in ballet class, hearing and remembering a correction is less than the minimum requirement. A dancer must hear, remember and then show through their dancing that improvement. Slacking in this delays development, and can kill a career.

IMPROVE EVERY DAY.

All dancers endeavor to continuously improve and aspire to an ever-increasing advance on the ultimate goals of artistry. The idea of mastering a step is a false notion. It is required that dancers learn the recipe of force to mechanically accomplish the various steps3, but just being able to do a step reliably is not an end but a beginning.

A dancer must always seek to improve, and indeed must actually improve. Quite often teachers will focus on the mechanics or techniques of a particular step (pirouettes, for example, are demanding and require constant work), and if a dancer does not truly engage the effort to improve every single day, they will focus only on the step. But dancing is not the steps; it is between the steps. How you transition from one foot to the other, from one step to the next, is where dancing lives. As a dancer works on the steps, the effort to constantly improve will ultimately reach beyond the boundaries of a step and reach into the dancing itself.

It is important to remember that choreography that is performed while based on standard academic steps, transforms the steps into a movement language that is unique. So since one never actually performs classroom steps on stage, it is important to constantly work to be able to add variances into the steps. These variances are sometimes small—a different arm for example. But often they are quite large. It is one thing to do a pirouette, and quite another to do a pirouette on one knee with the body in a changing shape during the turn. It is still a pirouette and the better you are at doing pirouettes the more you can apply that to the choreographed turn.

Constant improvement must be required of one's self. Certainly teachers and directors always demand it, but the only person who can achieve it is the dancer. And this means constantly working, not just in class, and not just in class when it is your turn to dance. One must work on things at every opportunity. This will give constant improvement.

---

3 Classical ballet has 284 distinct steps.

THE PERSON DANCING HAS THE RIGHT OF WAY.

For a dancer to do his or her very best takes absolute focus. To afford each person the best circumstance in which to fully apply their focus to their dancing, it is incumbent on others who are not dancing to give them right of way. Therefore, in a studio or on stage, if you are not dancing, then you must be certain you are not standing in the way of a dancer's path, or do not move into his/her path.

If two people collide in a studio, the one who is not dancing is at fault in all cases. When two people are both dancing, then see Rule 33.

WHEN PATHS CROSS, STAGE LEFT CROSSES DOWNSTAGE (IN FRONT).

Pursuant to Rule 32, when two dancers are both dancing, there is a rule that solves the problem, Rule 33. The rule, just like traffic lane laws and maritime navigation, is universally applied so that even a dancer who is just standing in on an emergency basis to participate can avoid collision with another dancer.

The rule could not be simpler, however there are exceptions. Some choreographic situations will call for the reversal of this rule, but that is only the case when, and if, the choreographer or rehearsal director discovers there is some reason for the reversal.

Otherwise, the dancer on stage left always crosses downstage of the dancer on stage right.

SECTION 4 - BODY RULES

There are nineteen (19) rules for the body in ballet. These rules accommodate balance, mobility, accessing and using forces and basic mechanics of the body. When used, dancing becomes more fluid and the dancer remains fully in control of his/her body at all times.

These do not come about to achieve some sort of stylistic 'look' or desired aesthetic related to a preference of some person in the past. They are not restrictions, or petty rules meant to control, punish or contain dancers. Nor are they intended to force a dancer to bend to the will of the director, choreographer or teacher. These rules make things easy, fluid, efficient and strong for the dancer. In fact, following these rules is indeed the easier, softer way – though they may be difficult to remember and/or do at first. Like everything else in dancing, it takes work and repetition to get these things incorporated into one's dancing.

Occasionally, as with most rules, there will be exceptions which usually make a great deal of kinetic sense, though sometimes they are a bit of a mystery why the exception. But always, in practice, the rule and the exception will always make dancing easier and better.

Some of these have their origin all the way back to the early Royal Courts of Europe, and indeed were not originally based on kinetic flow, balance or body needs. However, the very clever originators of ballet technique took these Royal peccadillos and incorporated them in such a way that they indeed helped the dancer dance, as well as followed the directive of the Monarch who insisted on them.

Enjoy learning these, for they are a true treasure for every dancer. In fact, these are a key that unlocks the ability of each dancer to dance one's very best at all times.

ÉPAULEMENT INCLINES THE HEAD TOWARD THE PUBLIC.

This rule emerged due to politics, patronage and conventions in the Royal Courts. However, the very first ballet masters, who originated the art form, cleverly conceded to these Royal whims in a way that is fundamental for the dancer. These whims were implemented as essential elements for maintaining balance and kinetic fluidity. And in addition, because of the origin of these elements, they give a dancer posture and regal bearing. This rule once applied facilitates movement, and allows expression to be readable even at a great distance from the stage.

Épaulement comes from deep within the dancer's upper torso, specifically just under the shoulder blade on one side or the other. This area of the body lifts upward and forward very slightly, with the shoulder remaining in its original place. The weight of the head falls slightly over that side of the body, and is caused to incline, as if you are listening to a tiny person or bird sitting on the top of the shoulder. But there is a rule within this rule:

Never turn your head.

To the public it will seem that you are moved from within, and are thinking wistfully about something or someone. It creates interest for the public, and allows them to relate. So long as the view of the dancer does not, with a turn of the head, look somewhere specific, the sense is internal—a memory, a notion, a feeling, a yearning, a fondness, etc. Épaulement is the evidence of the internal world of human feeling of the dancer, and the invitation to relate.

THE HEAD RISES THE SAME DISTANCE AS THE HEEL.

The simple logic of this rule is striking, yet it remains elusive to dancers, and particularly dancers newly on pointe. All dancers need to be reminded. Fear of loss of balance will make dancers sit heavily on their hips when they rise or spring up onto their extended foot or feet, as if staying close to the ground guarantees balance. Indeed, the opposite is true.

The fact is, when a dancer lifts up from the top of the head as they press down with the toes, the body lengthens and unites. This 'whole' feeling of the body allows the dancer to feel the entirety of their body as a single unit and is thereby more able to know when it is tilted, bent, twisted or in some other way fighting balance. Just like pulling the ends of a string in opposite directions lengthens the string, the same is true of the body when lifting up and pushing down simultaneously.

Beginning with this rule, it can then expand outward from there. The change in distance the feet go upward when leaving the floor must be matched by the top of the head and the body between. Doing this in a jump allows the dancer to shape the arc of movement in a jump, and also ride on top of that arc giving a lightness to the movement. And when an arc crests in a jump, there is a moment of stillness, as if the dancer is floating in the air. This only happens if the top of the body is lifting and shaping its course through the air in conjunction to the rest of the body.

THE HEAD INCLINES TOWARD THE SIDE WHERE THE FOOT ENDS IN FRONT

The ease of movement in dance is a vital element of dancing. The dancing posture is up and forward at an angle of 4.5° so that there is always a sense of movement, actual or anticipated. When ambulatory (or locomotive) steps are done (*glissade, chassé, tombé, pas de bourré*, etc.) they are meant to be transitory steps that connect the more demonstrative steps. These are the steps that connect a movement phrase. As the body moves, the feet pass through 5th position constantly (this is because in 5th position both feet are directly under the very center of the body so the body weight can be passed from one foot to the other along the way without lurching or bouncing from one foot to the other.

Each 5th position is the end of one step, which leads seamlessly to the next step. The body is dancing, has a slight forward tilt, and so must remain with the weight true to the dancing posture. When the head (weighing between 10-14 lbs. in a normal adult) is inclined toward the front foot it keeps the weight going in the desired direction. Lurching from foot to foot should the feet not transition directly below the body is not nearly as awkward as lurching forward and backward. And so, this rule maintains that smoothness.

But the head must incline toward the side of the body of which the foot will be in front at the end of the step, but it must do this at the very start of the step. And here it is meant the very start—as the body begins to move the head is instantly inclined—not at any other point during the movement.

EXCEPTIONS:

In *grand plié en 5me position au centre* the head inclines toward the back foot. This is true regardless of the body attitude (*croissé, éffacé,* or *en face*). This balances the body.

PLACE THE HEAD WHERE IT NEEDS TO BE, THE BODY WILL FOLLOW.

The mechanical aspect of ballet is most efficient when the whole body works as one. Leading with the head, placing it in the precise space it is to occupy at the completion of a movement allows the entire body to arrive in tact. This is efficient, reliable and gives the dancer maximum control.

The musical aspect of ballet calls for the dancer to place the body in a position, or into motion, on specific notes and phrases of the music. By placing the head where it needs to be so that the whole body arrives allows the dancer to decide precisely when this will happen. Thus the movement is entire, complete and is transformed into the visualization of the music. This is important all of the time, but is essential in works that are abstract or non-narrative driven. When the story is the visualization of music, then the dancer must dance in this precise manner.

DERIVATIONS:

► Know where you will arrive before you take off;
► Take the line you intend to take, at the location you choose to take it;
► Be there on the precise note of the music;
► Keep balanced

EXCEPTIONS:

► In dramatic works, use the placement and movement of the head to depict character;
► When the head lags behind or jumps forward it creates a kinetic sense of relationship to line, music and mood

"WHEN THE ARMS ACCOMPANY EACH MOVEMENT OF THE BODY WITH EXACTITUDE, THEY MAY BE COMPARED TO A FRAME THAT SETS OFF A PICTURE. BUT IF THE FRAME IS SO CONSTRUCTED AS NOT TO SUIT THE PAINTING, HOWEVER WELL EXECUTED THE LATTER MAY BE, ITS WHOLE EFFECT IS UNQUESTIONABLY DESTROYED.

"SO IT IS WITH THE DANCER; FOR WHATEVER GRACEFULNESS HE MAY DISPLAY IN THE PERFORMANCE OF HIS STEPS, UNLESS HIS ARMS BE LITHESOME AND IN STRICT HARMONY WITH HIS LEGS, HIS DANCE CAN HAVE NO SPIRIT NOR LIVELINESS, AND HE PRESENTS THE SAME INSIPID APPEARANCE AS A PAINTING WITHOUT ITS FRAME OR IN ONE NOT AT ALL ADAPTED TO IT."

IN BRAS BAS THE ARMS FALL TO GRAVITY

In ballet the inclusion of natural forces (gravity, momentum, torque, arrest) makes the most natural movements, which read to the audience as authentic. This authenticity also denotes human commonality, allowing the viewer to relate to the expressing being offered. Together, this human quality combined with authenticity of movement creates an integrity of dance performance that transcends the steps and allows the dancer, through the choreography, to speak to the public.

Arms frame the expression, complete the line, demonstrate intent and direct the eye. They also balance the body, or to the opposite effect cause the body to move out of a state of balance into another state. They are perhaps the most important part of expressing through dance. When the arm is dropping, letting gravity have the arm shows confidence that the dancer knows what they are doing, and that they are in accord and harmony with reality. In a passage that is soft or slow, still allow the weight of the arms to descend as gravity commands, but release the arm to gravity at the correct speed of flow.

A dropping arm, if not arrested at the bottom, will continue to swing as the arm is a pendulum and will gather momentum as it falls. You, the dancer, have absolute control of this even though you use gravity to cause the arm to fall.

DERIVATIONS:

- ▶ Anytime a body part is descending, let gravity do the work;
- ▶ Natural movements occur when the body works with the laws of physics and motion;
- ▶ The smoothest movement comes from allowing instead of forcing

EXCEPTIONS:

- ▶ Sharp, unnatural or robotic movements are achieved by not allowing gravity and momentum to participate;
- ▶ Forcing downward movement demonstrates authoritarian or erratic intention;
- ▶ When expressing an unnatural response or state of being, do not use gravity or momentum, use muscles instead.

ALL ARM MOVEMENTS ARE LED BY THE FINGERTIPS.

All movement of the arms must be led by the fingertips as a rule so that the movements are clear, efficient and have the most impact. This way of moving the arms keeps each arm as a single element. As a frame for position and motion, when the arms undulate or move without coordination, they become a broken visual frame. Arm movements led by the fingertips into or between positions, keep a strong visual frame.

When the arms are led by the fingertips, the emerging or changing line is inevitable, as the public can clearly see the movement and its likely objective. Having arrived at a line this way, it is easy to see, and reads as purposeful and 'meant to be', all the result of leading with the fingertips. Arm movements that undulate, seem broken and move without unity, are confusing to the eye, out of sync with the music, and are dismissed by the viewer as being unimportant—as if an arbitrary result rather than an intention with purpose.

When the arms move from the fingertips, then they also read as coming from within the dancer, so that their expression becomes authentic and believable as a statement.

DERIVATIONS:

► The fingertips reach outward as the arm moves, without changing the arc of the arm at the elbow;
► If the elbow angle is seen it is not classical

EXCEPTIONS:

► Softened or angular arms are choreography and design;
► To soften movement, the wrist has an allowable range of +/- 10° for a total range of 20°

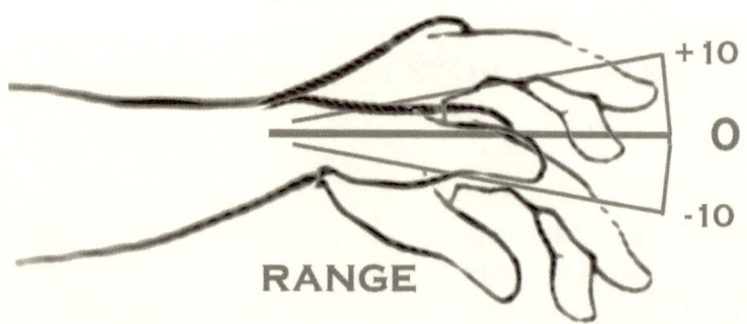

RANGE

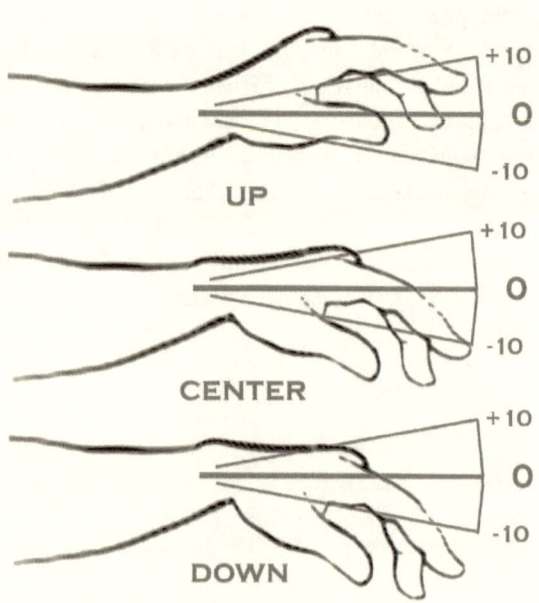

UP

CENTER

DOWN

ARMS COMPLETE THE LINE, FRAME EXPRESSION, BALANCE THE BODY, AND LEAD THE EYE OF THE AUDIENCE.

Arms frame the dance, lead the eye and express. They weigh 10° of the body, able to balance and create momentum. This rule is to serve as a constant reminder.

When the arms direct the eye as they complete the line of the body, there is a strong sense of purpose, as indeed line in ballet has. The choreographer uses them to shape space, and are painting a picture in space.

Classical theatrical dance is a profound means of universal expression, and the arms play a very large part here. Aside from the codified system of classical mime, or more contemporary uses of pedestrian gesture speaking to the public of its place in time, any expressive use of the arms is a fundamental part of why the dancing is happening at all.

DERIVATIONS:

► Arm movements must be mechanically efficient;
► Style is largely based in the arms;
► Gesture is speech, be careful what you say.

EXCEPTIONS:

► Depending on the statement, all rules for arms can go out the window;
► When arms are out of sync with movement the expression is about the forces at play rather than the intention of the dancer;
► Breaking the rules is sometimes the strongest statement.

AT THE BARRE THE SUPPORTING LEG REMAINS IN 1ST POSITION THROUGHOUT.

This rule comes from Enrico Cecchetti's book on technique. In fact, it is the final sentence of the entire section on barre work, and seems so simple that it might have been an afterthought. And yet, it is one of the most important principles of dance. This cannot be overemphasized, and it is absolutely literal. Standing in 1st position the body is evenly balanced between both legs, and both legs are at their tallest (any other position places the leg at an angle shortening the distance from the top of it to the floor. It all makes sense, and seems very simple.

As a practice this is tremendously challenging. Holding onto the relative position of standing leg to pelvis activates the gluteus medius and the IT band. These muscles once developed remain throughout life and change the posture and kinetic mobility of the body entirely. And in addition to activating those muscles, it also requires the psoas to work constantly—the psoas is the link between the lower and upper body, making the movement completely unified. And unified movement gives the dancer absolute control over where the body is and when it is there. This allows the dancer to achieve any musical phrasing and timing they would want. This produces refinement and the possibility of high level artistry.

DERIVATIONS:

- ▶ Balance is dynamic, not static;
- ▶ Balance toward the working leg;
- ▶ Always be able to move in any direction from where you are without having to move to the top of the standing leg first;
- ▶ Turnout and hip movement are the result of freedom from being weighed down;
- ▶ For dancers with hyperextended knees, the standing leg must be straight in alignment even if it feels like the knees are slightly bent;
- ▶ Lift on your hips.

EXCEPTIONS:

- ▶ When in 5th position relevé, and doing a movement that will return to that in the end, keep the angle of the standing leg in the originating 5th position;
- ▶ Choreography rules per Ballet's Second Rule – "the step is never wrong".

52

THE MUSCLES OF THE LEG LIFT THE LEG.

In the late 20th Century and into the 21st Century the norm for dancing became quite heavy, and dancers were trained to pay more attention to the distance of the leg/foot from the ground in positions, rather than the quality of movement or the integrity of alignment. There was also a fascination with the flexibility of the very young bodies of teenagers, and a pressure for students to achieve the 'look' of a step rather than actually doing the movement of the step. And this led to a blindness based on extension alone, subsequently establishing the very bad habit of lifting the legs with the hip and not with the muscles of the leg.

This practice is simply bad technique and has all sorts of ill effects on the dancing. When the leg is lifted to the front or *à la seconde* in accord with this rule, the sartorius muscle comes into play. It allows the leg to be lifted quite high without lifting the hip.

DERIVATIONS:

► Keep the lifted leg close;
► Lift the leg from the tip of the toes;
► Lift the spine and allow the leg to move freely and easily;
► Stand tall at the apex of the supporting leg.

EXCEPTIONS:

► In *penché à la seconde* the working leg lifts to its maximum and then the gluteus medias of the supporting leg activates to tilt the hips;
► Some off-centered movements require the lifting of the working hip with the leg;
► Movements that have their impetus in the torso will sometimes cause a hip to be thrown out, up, forward or back along with the leg.

A LEG EXTENDED DEVANT IS SUPPORTED BY THE LOWER BACK

This is one of the rules that is not a literal directive for mechanics or actual body position and use. It is a directive for thinking or mind frame to which the body responds with the correct coordination of muscles to activate properly. The literal aspect of this is that the psoas muscle does come into use, and when it does the feeling of lifting the leg to the front indeed is in the lower back.

The body response to this is tremendous. The knee caps lift in a way that lengthens the leg, the sartorius activates and rotates the leg. This puts the heel forward and gives the feeling that the closer you bring your leg to you, the higher it lifts to the front. This increases the energy in the lift of the leg with any step that involves *grand battement en avant.*

This rule, when applied, lifts the leg and improves the lift of the upper torso. It also frees the dancer to be able to do any choreography with arm and upper body movements while maintaining balance and freedom of movement.

DERIVATIONS:

- ▶ Meet your leg with your chest and clavicles up and forward in space;
- ▶ Lift your naval up and into the front of your spine;
- ▶ Relax your quadriceps and allow them to fall to gravity on the outside of the leg;
- ▶ Keep your heel forward as if you could set something on the inside surface of it;
- ▶ Point to the tips of your toes.

EXCEPTIONS:

- ▶ None.

WHEN ONE LEG CHANGES SIDE OF THE BODY THE TOE LIFTS ½ INCH

This rule is literal, and gives a natural flow to this type of leg movement. It is hard for most dancers to limit the lift to just ½" and not lift it further. Usually this happens because they have used the hip to initiate the leg movement, and when that hip falls back into properly placed alignment the leg suddenly jumps up higher than planned.

The language of dance is a visual language that is related to emotions. When the leg is lifted to the front, it is about going somewhere and has the sense of becoming elevated. As the leg travels *à la seconde* it lifts just ½" only, which speaks of something continuing rather than arriving in a static place. Should it continue to arabesque, it lifts another ½" so that it has the sense of having arrived. This is also true en dedans.

This rule is about trajectory, eventuality and approaching some sort of fulfillment. It also forces the body to work as an integrated whole. This is compelling for the public and allows control and artistry.

DERIVATIONS:

- ▶ Dance beyond the limitations of the physical body, speaking of limitless potential of expression;
- ▶ Work with the whole body;
- ▶ Know where you will end and how you will get there;
- ▶ Forward is your friend.

EXCEPTIONS:

- ▶ When expressing a non-human element, keep the level of the leg the same;
- ▶ In contemporary works lift beyond this rule to maximum expressiveness where appropriate.

RULE 45: FORWARD LEG MOVEMENT

WHEN THE LEG MOVES FORWARD THE HEEL LEADS.

Maintaining turnout is essential in ballet, and is intrinsically related to placement. It is these two – turnout and placement – that create and sustain stability. At first look, this rule is very clear in that moving the leg forward through or from a static foot position will assure that the leg is turned out.

It also means that *only* the heel leads, leaving the hips still and stable in the process. It is easy to produce the look of the heel leading by twisting the hips, and dropping the working hip behind the standing hip. But only when the hips remain still and strong, with the heel leading the leg forward, are both turnout and placement achieved and maintained.

In addition, leading means going first, and indeed, the heel's forward movement is the impetus of all forward movements of the leg. The timing aspect of the leadership of the heel speaks to the greater involvement of specific muscles from the start of a movement. While it is possible for the leg to be moved forward with an initial forward thrust of the hip and only later bringing the heel forward, it upsets the placement (and therefore balance) of movement and position.

If ballet were a sport, or merely an athletic pursuit, approximate movement would suffice so long as the point was scored in the game. However, it is a fine art form, and refinement at all times is required as a minimum. Things must be done properly or not at all in ballet, and the movement of every dancer must be refined, authentic and have integrity. The end result is seen in the quality of the movement, rather than the mere fact of it. And quality of movement is what makes ballet a high art form, elevating it far above entertainment and effect.

DERIVATIONS:

► Keep your heel forward;
► Lead with the heel each time the foot addresses the floor;
► Knee to the ceiling, Heel forward.

EXCEPTIONS:

► Stylized choreography may contradict this rule;
► Ballet versions of folk and national dances sometimes break this rule;
► In Modern and Contemporary dance the rule is secondary to other considerations and focuses.

WHEN THE LEG MOVES BACKWARD THE TOE LEADS.

One of the most difficult things to coordinate, particularly for the student who is younger than 12 or 13 years, is to initiate a backward movement of the leg from the toe. It requires the use of the piriformis in conjunction to other muscles that feels like an isolation exercise at the start. Once the muscles are strong, and the piriformis is developed, this becomes easier.

It is also very difficult to coordinate this movement without leading with the working hip and relaxing the knee of the working leg. The Rotation Exercise[4] is very helpful in preparing the body for this aspect of ballet. This rule keeps the leg turned out as it moves away from the front.

By keeping the focus on the toes, the whole leg automatically engages, and it isolates if from movements of the hips. This combination of results from simply paying attention to the toe leading the leg is very efficient. It simplifies the many complex elements of doing this movement.

DERIVATIONS:

- ▶ Turnout the leg to the back;
- ▶ Keep your hips square as you move the leg backwards;
- ▶ Keep the leg close to you;
- ▶ Feel the line of the leg behind you.

EXCEPTIONS:

- ▶ None.

---

4 See the Academy Method: Body Mechanics textbook.

PUSH DOWN WITH THE BIG TOE TO CAUSE THE LEG TO OPEN.

Even though one is to "use the muscles of the leg to move the leg" as a rule, the very initiation of that movement begins with the tip of the big toe. Downward pressure of the tip of the big toe used to cause the leg to open from any closed position or stance puts into effect several very important things.

First, for this downward pressure to translate into an opening of the leg, the rest of the body must remain unified, except for the hip of the working leg. The contrast between the unity of the entire body and one relaxed hip allows the opening of the leg to commence with ease and without upsetting the alignment (placement) of the rest of the body.

Second, this approach activates the psoas on the working side, so that the resulting leg movement indeed comes from within the body. When movement comes from within and is thereby the result of some inner catalyst, it becomes expressive and authentic when viewed.

Third, initiating the movement thus, the dancer is not likely to rely on the hip to continue the leg movement, but rather on the muscles of the active leg. This allows the dancer the full range of movement, and the full measure of power, the working leg has potential for.

Forth, finally, when the leg opens the entire foot must point, without breaking at the ball of the foot (which pulls the dancer off balance and upsets placement). By teaching the foot to fire all of its joints simultaneously, the maximum power is achieved.

DERIVATIONS:

► Maintain placement as the leg opens;
► Do not let the movement of the leg cause any other part of the body to move;
► Point the whole foot at once;
► Use the muscles of the leg to move the leg.

EXCEPTIONS:

► Lifting the leg into a position with the knee bent does not use this;
► In *chassé*, the body moves with the opening leg, staying with the moving foot as it moves, and in this the sense is that the heel initiates the movement and the ball of the foot is relaxed as it takes the weight of the body.

IN À LA SECONDE BRING BOTH HIP AND HEEL OF THE WORKING LEG FORWARD.

This rule, while true from the start, is not introduced to dancers until they are will progressed in puberty. With this phase of development, the tendons and ligaments around the pelvis begin to form their adult attachment to the skeletal structure, leading the dancer to a moment we call "finding the legs". Until the pelvic area has begun to mature, it is nearly impossible for the dancer to feel the unity between the torso and the legs. Once it is clear that the dancer has "found the legs" then this rule can be applied.

The complex mechanical system that comes into play with the leg placed *à la seconde* involves many, many muscles. It is impossible for the human mind to monitor all of these simultaneously. Yet, with the idea "bring hip and heel forward" as the active focus, the entire system works.

So much of dancing is about efficiency. One must be efficient with energy so that their energy can be maintained throughout any length of dancing passage. One must be efficient throughout the day so that all of life can be achieved and maintained even when supporting the large daily time commitment dancing requires. One must be efficient with muscle use so that quick movements are possible, and so that all ambulatory movement is fluid and in harmony. One must be efficient with expended energy so there is ample energy to apply to phrasing, expression, dramatic pacing and character arc. And one must be efficient with use of the body so that injury is avoided in the short term, and the dancer's career achieves longevity. This rule condenses a complex system into one efficient focus.

DERIVATIONS:

► Keep your leg close to you;
► In *à la seconde* the sole of the foot faces front;
► Do not lift the hip or let it drop back.

EXCEPTIONS:

► None.

GET YOUR HEEL FORWARD.

This rule is perhaps the instruction most given in Academy Method classes. It is truly a fundamental element at the foundation of all classical dancing. It refers to three different ways in which one can "get your heel forward" all of which are essential.

First, it refers to the shape of the foot on the ankle. To properly point the foot one uses the *fibular longus* muscle to extend the ankle, and then the *flexor digitori* muscles to point the toes. This coordination places the foot into a structural balance with the center of the ankle directly aligned with the second toe of the foot, a balance that requires few other muscles to maintain. In addition, fully extending the foot in this way does not involve the *gastrocnemius* nor the Achilles tendon, making it efficient and avoiding stressing the Achilles when landing. This ankle shape and muscle coordination is the same as in the *sur le cou de pied* position.

The second way of getting the heel forward is by turning out the leg. When the leg is rotated it naturally brings the heel forward in terms of the front of the body. Turnout is stability for dancers, and is one of the qualities even the public can understand and see.

The third way to bring the heel forward is quite literally to move the leg toward the front, so that the heel is brought forward. This only applies in some movements.

Usually this rule refers to the shape of the foot, and is a preventative to injury, gives a very natural balance ability, and creates the most aesthetic visual line in the body.

DERIVATIONS:

- ► The second toe aligns with the center of the ankle;
- ► Maintain turnout;
- ► Shape the foot;
- ► Relax the Achilles tendon when landing.

EXCEPTIONS:

- ► Some teachers insist on an overstretched instep, which causes the toe to sickle and is not a proper line, also being weak.

LIFT YOUR HIPS.

This rule is literal, but cannot be achieved until mid- to late-teenage in terms of skeletal and muscular development. It is a physical reality that the human body can, when developed properly, actually lift the pelvis and upper body up off of the hips about ½" upward. Technically this is because of the simultaneous engagement of the psoas, erector spine muscles, and several other sets of muscles. By lifting the hips up this way, the legs are free to gain their full power and to completely rotate in the hip socket. However, just hearing this is not enough.

When the direction "lift your hips" is given from early on in a dance student's training, they will try to do what they understand this would mean. Continuing to do this, and also being told to have "soft" or "silent" landings creates the proper mindset in the student.

Then, by the age of 15-16 the body has developed adequately that the skeleton and muscles can start to lift the weight of the torso and upper body, as well as the pelvis, up off of the legs. And by the age of 19-21 the dancer will be able to intentionally lift the pelvis off of the legs.

DERIVATIONS:

► The deeper the *demi-plié* the higher the torso lifts up;
► Lift up when landing jumps;
► In very rapid petit allegro jumps, the toes only lift a paper-width from the floor and there is no *demi-plié* used;
► *Ballon* is the result of being lifted on the hips throughout a jumping passage;
► Don't drop weight into the hip in preparations or landings;
► Up is down, down is up;
► In a *piquet* lift from the top of the head so that the body is in the air above the length of the extended leg, and the upward motion is caught at the apex without any sort of 'landing' or coming back down onto the new supporting leg;
► Lift up and forward from the top of the head.

EXCEPTIONS:

► When the torso is being used as a generator of force, then dropping the weight into the hips in the preparation is appropriate;
► Low, deep *plié* without a lift in the hips is an important statement in choreographic expression, in juxtaposition to the normal state of lifted hips it becomes more powerful and evident.

FOR PASSÉ SIMULTANEOUSLY LIFT KNEE TO CEILING AND HEEL FORWARD.

There is a balance in motion when the working leg bends, or any time it goes into a *passé* position, regardless if that position is an ending point or within a transitional movement. By simultaneously lifting the knee to the ceiling (directly upward from where it begins) and rotating the heel forward (with the shape of the foot in relation to the lower leg and ankle, as well as turnout), the body experiences the same balanced state throughout. It is like a dew-point where there is constant fluidity but perpetual balance.

These dual forces must be done absolutely simultaneously, and from the very initiation of the movement. For the knee this means that it lifts directly upward toward the ceiling from wherever it is. One does not 'turn out' the knee or upper thigh, but simply lift it directly upward. For the foot, it means that the heel moves forward as the toe moves backward taking the proper alignment with the center of the ankle in line with the second toe, and then continue with the emphasis on the heel coming forward in all ways relevant.

The result is a smooth mechanical transition into *passé* from whatever position one begins in. Since many *pirouettes* are done in the *passé* position, this rule is fundamental to establishing an easy balance for the turns. It is also a tremendous advantage for prolonged adage work, and for body transitions while being partnered. There cannot be enough emphasis on the repeated practice of this rule so that the movement becomes automatic, for it stabilizes overall dancing.

DERIVATIONS:

▶ Moving the foot from standing position to *sur le cou de pied* must begin with the heel moving forward as the toe moves backward, both heading directly to their finishing point;

▶ Use *grand battement passé* at the start of *pirouettes* to lift the pelvis upward and establish an easy balance at the start of the turn.

EXCEPTIONS:

▶ None.

THE STRONGER THE MUSCLES, THE LESS FLEXIBLE THE JOINT.

As logical as this rule seems, it is sometimes hard to know precisely how to apply it. One must strengthen muscles to dance, and one must be flexible to dance. Dancers spend thousands of hours per year working alternately on strength and stretch. So why does this become a rule?

This is a rule because often a dancer overworks a correction, or focuses too much on one area of weakness, not realizing that the constant strengthening of muscles can cause other problems if not done equitably and carefully. Weight training is not recommended for classical dancers, for example, because building too much muscle bulk will block the flexibility of the joints. When a joint's flexibility is inhibited by over-strong muscles it alters the line of the body, and interrupts kinetic flow.

Beyond this there is another consideration. Efficiency of movement in dance is an ultimate goal. By allowing gravity, torque, rebound, pendular swing and other natural forces to do the work instead of muscles wherever possible makes for fluid dancing, prevents injuries and prolongs the dancing years of a career.

When there is a "weakness" it doesn't always mean the muscles are weak. It can mean that a position has not been achieved with a natural flow and the sudden use of muscles to hold the position upset the balance, for example. Always check with your Ballet Master, coach, director, or an accomplished fellow dancer to be sure you are not overdoing it.

DERIVATIONS:

▶   The less the muscles dominate a movement the quicker it is;
▶   Bulky muscles work against classical dancing;
▶   Skeletal balance is preferred over muscular tension.

EXCEPTIONS:

▶   None.

SECTION 5 – MOVEMENT RULES

The movement rules in ballet are quite exciting to discover and work with. They make sense of ballet movement, and show that classical dancing and classical line need not be unnatural for the body. The rules in this section take into account the laws of physics, the fundamental principles of motion as they apply to classical theatrical dancing, and the way in which the human body actually functions.

The aesthetic line of ballet is impressive. To see a body in complete harmony with each part doing its absolute maximum simultaneously creates such a compelling phenomenon that it is sought by all ballet students. Yet to simply force the body into a position, without knowing the rules for moving the body, results in injury, awkward movement, and lack of coordination.

Dancing is found between the positions, not in the positions. It is also between the steps, how a dance artist phrases and blends one step to the next. This is the basis of dancing, and it is where artistry and expression come from.

In this section, take the movement rules quite seriously. They are the 'keys to the kingdom' when followed. Margot Fonteyn advised teachers to "teach what you know is true of movement from having done it—no theories or philosophies." She said this based on her historic career—both in length and artistic scope—as she worked with many companies and in many systems of ballet. It was this belief of hers that led her to compiling the Academy Method.

The human body is brilliant. Its design allows for levels of artistry in motion that no other species is capable of. And while each body differs in proportion, shape, temperament and kinetic individuality, they all share the facts from nature and physics. In this section the rules of motion are given and explained. These rules are treasures for every dancer.

IT TAKES 100,000 REPETITIONS FOR A MOVEMENT TO BECOME AUTOMATIC.

This is a fact that holds great significance to classical dance. The movements at the barre train the muscles to work in particular combinations, and give the muscles a particular shape. In training a dancer it is absolutely essential to use repetition so that basic fundamental movements (e.g., *tendu, pliè, ronde de jambe, grand battement, dégagé, frappé,* etc.) become automatic by the 4th or 5th year of study. As soon as this happens, the young dancer begins to emerge. As the body grows, reaches maturity, and the dancer learns more and more of the steps of ballet, they will be refined and instantly recognizable as a classical dancer.

This rule reaches beyond the physical mechanics of the body. Classical ballet came from a long tradition from within the Royal Courts of Europe. These traditions must be automatic as well. The stances of body attitude, conventions of the arms, use of the upper body, and way in which various groups of people interact (such as teacher/student, director/stage manager, choreographer/dancer, etc.) must also become automatic. There are many traditions in ballet that are not written, and only those who grow up within the ballet world will understand them. This is why mixing commercial dancers and classical dancers rarely works at all well.

This rule also speaks to habits, both good and bad, that dancers develop. One must be ever vigilant to be sure that some shortcut or adaptation is not practiced enough to become automatic. The very reason that dancers are corrected repeatedly from the very start of their training is so that no quirk, habit or peculiarity is allowed to pass the eye of the teacher without being caught and set right.

Listen to every correction given, and remember it. Constantly watch other dancers and learn. Watch video and film of great dancers endlessly, particularly those from before the 1980s when training was thorough, and no shortcuts were allowed.

Never balk at practicing, and make sure you practice every transition as much as you practice the steps on either side of a transition. It takes tenacity and diligence to become a beginning dancer, and even more after that. Remember this is a high minded, refined, sophisticated fine art form.

USE NATURAL FORCES INSTEAD OF MUSCLES.

Use gravity, rebound, friction, momentum and other elements of physics to create absolute efficiency of movement and economy of body energy.

Physical bodies fall at 32'/secs. This means that if you were to hold your leg at hip height (probably about 3' from the ground) and completely relax it but nothing else. It would be in 1st position in .09 seconds. There is no muscle movement that can bring the leg down to the ground quicker than that. In fact, all possible muscle movements to cause that would take significantly more time.

Whenever any part of the body is dropping quickly to the ground, the quickest way to get it there is by simply relaxing it. This saves a great deal of energy. And if we suppose that 50% of our movements go downward, and 50% go upwards, that is a total energy saving of 50%! But it is better than that because of the effects of rebound (or bounce), momentum (stored energy) and pendulum swing. If you drop a ball, just drop it and not throw it down, it will rebound to approximately ½ the height from which it was dropped. If you let something swing in a pendulum motion (like *balançois*) it will swing back upwards to almost 80% of the height from which it began to swing.

Taken all together, without considering momentum, any time you drop your arm, leg, torso, shoulder, etc., if you simply let gravity and physics do their job then you will save on average 75% of the muscle energy used to cause that to happen yourself.

This savings in energy is then able to be used elsewhere. You can put energy into phrasing, save wear and tear on your muscles, build your character, and many more things. People who use this will extend their careers and have much more pliable muscles.

<u>*DERIVATIONS:*</u>

▶   Don't make it happen, let it happen.

<u>*EXCEPTIONS:*</u>

▶   None.

---

5 The actual law of Newtonian physics states that physical matter falls at 32'/sec/sec, meaning that it falls further for every second it is falling. But since nothing in dance involves any part of the body, or the whole body, falling further than 32', we have simplified it for the ballet rule.

GOING UP, THE TOP OF THE HEAD LEADS; THE KNEECAPS ARRIVE FIRST.

It is important to employ psychology when working with the body. A human body is so complicated, timing of a complex coordination patterns is down to hundredths or thousandths of seconds, and factoring in cumulative effects of outside and internal forces, that it is impossible for even a super computer to make all of the calculations necessary to do any ballet step, much less a phrase of choreography. But, there are certain thoughts6 that cause this natural process to happen more efficiently.

In this case, when going upward it is important to actively lift upward with the whole body, not just one part, or pushing the weight of the body upward with legs or feet. Add to that the fact that when movements are doing simultaneously the energy, or power, of each is multiplied by the others, where movements done in sequence only have that energy added to the others.

When the body receives the message to lead with the top of the head, automatically all muscles south of that work together to lift up, but not necessarily at the same time. So when the body also receives the message that the kneecaps are to arrive first, this makes all of that lifting happen at precisely the same time, making the full body energy coordinated, and multiplied together. This allows the dancer to jump, rise, *relevé* or travel in an arc much more effectively and efficiently. It allows *batterie* to be free and clean, because the body is airborne longer.

DERIVATIONS:

▶ Be on the music;
▶ Express freely without showing the mechanics of the movement.

EXCEPTIONS:

▶ None.

---

6 "The Inner Game of Tennis: The Classic Guide to the Mental Side of Peak Performance" by W. Timothy Gallwey, first published 1974, Random House— presents the relationship between the mind and psychology and performance of physical tasks in a way that is clear and easy to apply to ballet.

BALANCE TOWARD THE WORKING LEG.

This rule runs counter to much of what is taught. In fact, until it has been attempted for quite some time, it is impossible to do, because only by attempting it does the body develop the muscle strength to do it. Like skills in sports (dribbling a basketball, passing a football, swinging a golf club, etc.) which must be practiced for years sometimes before the body develops the proper muscles to actually do the action, this is an essential skill. Yet, the pressure to win competitions based mainly on external and shallow impressions of technical form, cause teachers to ignore this entirely. In a sport the goal is to make the point, or arrive at the base.

In ballet, the visible goal is to balance. But here this is not about simply balancing (which can be achieved through tension, sitting heavily on the supporting let, or many other ways), but about balancing in a way that is at the full apex of the supporting leg, and allows the dancer to move fluidly in any direction, and after doing whatever is required while at the apex.

Mechanically, the pelvis is supported by only one leg and can only remain level when the many muscles of the supporting hip are engaged. In this case, the primary one is the gluteus medias, in conjunction with a very strong I/T band. It takes a huge amount of practice for the gluteus medias to strengthen adequately to maintain a level pelvis (and support the weight of the working leg at the same time) when balanced on one leg. But it is a fundamental goal to make dancing natural, smooth, and give the dancer the certainty of balance plus the freedom to craft each movement with artistry and musicality as they are required to do in public performance.

DERIVATIONS:

► Emphasis is on the world "balance toward" the working leg, not "fall off of" the working leg;
► Be on the very top of your leg;
► The standing leg must be perfectly vertical to be the tallest it can be;
► Work from 1st position, with the standing leg always in 1st position.

EXCEPTIONS:

► For stylized work, or when demanded by choreography, this rule may be disallowed, instance by instance.

KNOW WHERE YOU WILL LAND BEFORE YOU TAKE OFF.

Margot Fonteyn along with fellow ballerinas Sallie Wilson, Carmen Mathé, Eleanor D'Antuono and many others, have always cautioned against what they call "chance dance." In a classical fine art form it is imperative to have precision and control. Indeed, if the dancer is not sure what, when, how, when or sometimes if they will do a step, then how can they give an artistic rendering of that step? How can they plan their form and timing as an artistic expression that comes from them? In fact, if dancers just hope for the best, then you are not seeing technique at all, but just dumb luck.

In crafting a jump much more is happening than simply the body shape at the apex. The body is traveling in an arc across space, and with specific timing, and rhythm. Furthermore, the shape of the arc is part of the visual picture of the phrase of the movement, and where it takes off and where it ends are the definitions of that arc. Beyond these concerns, there is the visual line of the movement and the shape of the body complementing that visual line. Without knowing where, and in what position, you will land before taking off for a jump, it is impossible to have any control over all of these concerns. The shape of the body at the apex is just one part, though a very important one. But if what comes before and after is messy, arbitrary or disorganized then the entire jump is lackluster, and flat no matter what sparkle there may have been in the air.

DERIVATIONS:

▶ Move through the air as a unified body;
▶ Express the choreographic intent of the movement seamlessly with the artistic refinement;
▶ Do not jump unless you know where, when, and how you will land.

EXCEPTIONS:

▶ None.

RULE 58: STRUCTURAL COLLAPSE

BREAKING YOUR POSITION KILLS MOMENTUM.

This is quite simple. If you are turning in a pirouette and you suddenly let an arm fling out to one side, it kills the spin momentum (torque) and kills the *pirouette*. If you are sailing through the air in splits, and land with a collapse onto your hip or breaking the line of your back, it kills the momentum of the jump and destroys the arc. If you go into the air in a smooth uplifting motion and then jerk your head, arms, ribs or some other part, it kills the momentum of the jump and makes it much more likely it will result in a fall, a pulled muscle, or some other mess.

Likewise, if you are turning in a pirouette and hold onto the position with tension, then you can't stop, and will not be able to control where you are facing when you land. Or, in this same case, you may land facing front, but then the body will twist because there is too much momentum still at play in the body. Similarly, when you do a circular jump onto one leg (say in a *piquet* turn, or *coupé jeté en tournant*, etc.) and hold tension in your entire body, it will cause you to roll or spin out of control.

These are the two sides of this rule. As a dancer you must decide what you are going to do, as well as how, where, when and how much. Knowing that structural collapse (the sudden letting go of any joint of the body by relaxing it entirely and quickly) will siphon off the momentum of the body, gives an important tool to the dancing.

<u>*DERIVATIONS:*</u>

► A pirouette stops at the end of the turn when you are still up on your supporting leg, coming down from it is the start of the next step, not the end of the turn;
► When you land, hold the position, but relax the *demi-pliè*;
► In demi pliè do not drop in the hip, but have the heel down.

<u>*EXCEPTIONS:*</u>

► None.

WHEN A LIMB MOTION IS STOPPED, MOMENTUM TRAVELS TO THE CENTER.

Anytime movement of a body part is arrested, the momentum force of that body part will transfer so long as the full position of the body is maintained. In this case, it is not a relaxing of the joint (which causes structural collapse) but a halting of the motion in a fixed position. Springing onto pointe and simultaneously taking the working leg from *4ᵐᵉ devant* to *à la seconde*, and holding that position, will cause the entire body to turn on its axis. This is the fundamental mechanic of *tour à la seconde* and *fouetté en tournant*.

This rule is found throughout all of classical ballet, and can be effectively put to use with all forms of choreography, and even in sports. Such a fundamental principle of physics is very important for the dancer to remember. Without this, so many steps become confusing to learn and seem impossible for the student to achieve in fledgling attempts.

It is sometimes taught to young students in an exercise called the "Velcro Frisbee" in which the student holds a disk (an actual frisbee works perfectly) and then must do the movement of throwing it very far, starting with the frisbee brought to the center of the chest with the arm curved around it, and then unfurl the arm to straight in an opening movement. But instead of letting go of the frisbee, instead the student rises onto one foot and holds the arm and shoulder of the working side in a fixed position. This causes the student to spin on one foot with the arm and frisbee extended.

DERIVATIONS:

▶   Arms open in second position before chassé in new direction;
▶   *Relevé fouetté en promenade.*

EXCEPTIONS:

▶   None.

71

SECTION 6 – COORDINATION RULES

Fluid movement of dancing is all about coordination. Seamlessly going from one movement to the next, blending a turn into a promenade into an ambulatory step, etc. All is coordination.

The same is true of the coordination of body parts. Maintaining turnout while walking takes coordination as fundamentally as doing a *pirouette* does. And there are rules of coordination that give the dancer the ability to make artistic choices, expressive choices, musical choices and technical choices.

These rules are often about sequence within a coordination of movement. If the correct impetus for a movement is created, then the movement has greater quality. Since we are dealing with a fine art form, quality of movement becomes a foundational means of expression. In a sport it often doesn't matter about the quality of the movement, so long as the ball gets where it needs to be. Here it is the opposite. If the quality of the movement is not there, then it doesn't matter what the end result is.

These rules are very specific, and most of them only apply to precise situations and none other. Our approach to this section then will be different. There will be no "Derivations" or "Exceptions" listed. Instead, an discussion of the elements involved and the conditions in which the rule applies are presented with each rule.

Within the Rules of Coordination there are the following categories:

Rules of Force
Rules of Arrival
Rules of Ambulation
Rules of Effect

In this section each of these categories is discussed individually, and then the related rules follow that general discussion.

RULES OF FORCE

The first of the Coordination Rules are the Rules of Force. Each ballet step is simply a recipe of the forces employed by the dancer to execute movement. Whenever there is a natural force available—gravitational, rebound, pendulum swing, arrest—then that force is used to its utmost. There are also forces generated by the dancer—lift, thrust, momentum, torque, disbursal—that are applied as needed, and the dancer must learn exactly how much effort produces how much of the force.

Once the dancer understands which forces are to be used for a movement sequence, they then must learn the interrelationship between the forces in the recipe. Just like in cooking with a recipe, there is the ingredient list, and then the method of combining the ingredients. Just because egg, butter, milk, salt, flour, sugar, vanilla and leavening are in the bowl, they will produce a cake if combined one way, a pudding if another, a cookie if yet another, or a total mess in another.

These Rules of Force are about how and when to use the forces in combination to create the desired effect. It is the job of the dancer to perform choreography accurately, in a technically sound way, musically and as expressively as possible. All of this is called artistry, and ballet is a fine art form. Making critical decisions begins with performing steps cleanly and strongly. By applying the rules of force, this is possible.

IN SEQUENTIAL MOVEMENTS THE FORCES ARE ADDED

When movements are done sequentially (first one, then the next, etc.) the power of each is added to the power of the preceding one. Like stacking blocks on top of each other. Sometimes this is the right thing to do.

Imagine the heavy weight lifter in the Olympics. First, bending down and grasping the iron bar between the weights, there is a thrust that gets them up to the chest, knees bent. Then, with another thrust, the knees and then arms straighten lifting it above the head. This sequential use of force is the proper way to do this movement.

The relationship between the parts is called "additive" or, in mathematical terms, "arithmatic." It simply means each is done in sequence to achieve the result. Many Adage passages are built this way in ballet. And the overall structure of the barre's early exercises follow this design. By separating each elemental movement, the maximum force is developed.

More importantly, each individual force is felt by the dancer, and challenged by the muscles. This allows the dancer to maximize force, and be intimately familiar with the entire feeling of each movement.

In performance, this rule is often applied to create a building intensity in repeated movements. In many Romantic ballets, solos are built this way, since the Romantic Era explored what was to come, what was yearned for, and what was the outcome of events and feelings. You will often find a series of *relevés* in which the arm, leg fingers, or even head will lift higher each time it is repeated. By repeating a movement, but isolating the increases of impact of one body part, the mounting expectation for what is next becomes the imagery of dreaming, yearning, seeking and striving.

So too, is this additive progression often done in partnering. It is a show of force, and symbolic of ever intensifying accomplishment to the heights, to glory. Ballet is majestic, and this is one of the rules that, when applied, demonstrates that majesty.

IN SIMULTANEOUS MOVEMENTS THE FORCES ARE MULTIPLIED

This rule truly is ballet magic. All of the stretching, thousands of hours of training, endless rehearsals and coaching sessions produce the body that is capable of magic, but not the magic itself. The things that people say, in astonishment, praising the Ballet Gods and Goddesses of the stage in each generation all spring from the application of this rule: "He just hung in the air!"; "She suddenly was spinning like a top, from nowhere!"; "They all turned and it was like I was transported into another dimension!"; etc.

It is a simple law of physics that simultaneously applied forces are multiplied by each other. When the entire body fires muscles at the same precise instant, the resulting force is very far greater than the sum of its parts.

Consider the illustration below:

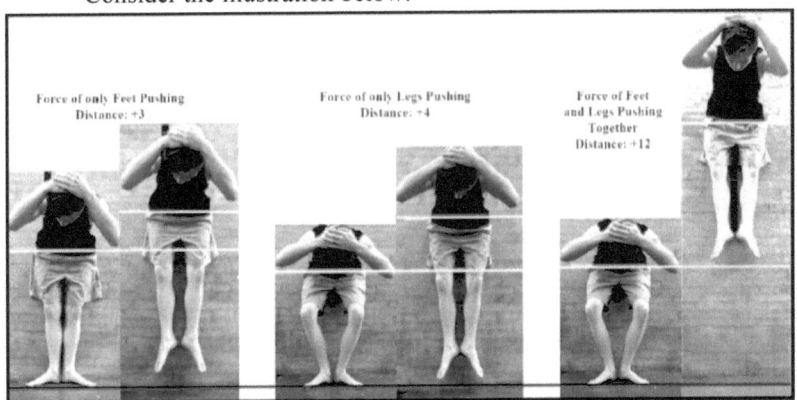

In this illustration, you see that an untrained person, by combing the force of push of the feet and legs at the same time multiplies the forces involved. Now, translate this into ballet...

When a dancer fires the push from a *demi-plié*, the force of a *frappé*, the lift of the arms and torso, and the lifting power of a *grand battement*, the result is a *grand jeté* with spectacular lift, hang time, and a beautiful arc. And this is then where the stretching and shaping of the body amplify the result into something quite magical, and super human seeming to the viewers.

And so this rule is the Magic of Ballet!

THE IMPETUS FOR EN DEHORS IS A LIFT UP AND FORWARD

When an arm or a leg is moving from front to back in a circular motion, the body must rebalance itself due to the shift of weight. Visually, this motion, regardless of it being done by an arm or a leg, demonstrates an openness and welcoming of what is coming. Since the body is already in a dancing posture when this is done, the ending distribution of weight will be well forward[7] of that initial forward incline, but will be in a balanced state. The challenge is making this transition smoothly and naturally.

By initiating this movement with a lift up and forward of the uppermost clavicle joints, placing them into their final relative alignment to the body, it creates the flow of natural movement, and demonstrates that this new position is inevitable.

This is very difficult for highly trained dancers to grasp if it has not been part of their initial training. Often dancers sit back in their weight, and use the hip to move the leg instead of the leg muscles. This makes them get stuck when the leg arrives *à la seconde* and they have to lurch forward, or pop their ribs out so the hip can carry the leg to the *arabesque* position. The resulting movement is awkward, non-aesthetic, and inexpressive. In fact, it tells the viewer that the dancer is struggling, the step is hard for them, and they are dealing only with managing their body mechanics and are no longer dancing. A total failure of effort.

Indeed, this rule makes the transition smooth and natural. And in times when the *en dehors* movement is quick, without this rule the result is unachievable.

---

7 The amount of the forward balance point for the weight of a leg is far greater than that of an arm.

IMPETUS FOR EN DEDANS—LEAD WITH THE HEEL

The quality of movement when bringing the leg forward from an arabesque alignment is determined by how the movement starts. For however it does start initiates a sequence of muscle involvement unique to that initiation. And the result will set the quality of movement and placement of the body until it reaches *à la seconde*. At this point, the body can correct any misalignment that has occurred in the execution of this leg movement. Of course, the need to change midway is the very definition of awkward or non-fluid movement.

Consider the impetus options here; there are only three: hip carrying leg, quadriceps bringing the leg around in parallel position, or the heel being rotated forward from the start. It is only by using the heel to initiate this movement that it can be done without misaligning the hips, maintaining turnout, and keeping proper placement. Thus, the existence of this rule.

A full *ronde de jambe en dedans* ends in 4me *devant*, and the movement is meant to be a smooth continuous flow from start to finish. When done properly it is a very significant movement that expresses a shift from the desire for something ahead to the commitment to it as a goal. This is the abstract meaning, and is there regardless of any direct correlation to a narrative plot or something literal. It just represents, in pure movement, that transition from yearning to establishing a goal. As such, if there is no flow, if it is interrupted midway, then that universal statement is lost.

The same is true of the visual line. The leg comes from behind in a smooth arc and ends in the front. This connects the focal point of the eyes at the start with the leg at the end. Again, if the arc is not smooth, the visual line and its visual statement are lost.

Adhere to this rule and your dancing becomes more focused, your placement more solid, and your ability to express heightened.

OPENING THE ARMS BALANCES FORWARD MOVEMENT

The dancing posture is lifted and forward, even when at rest. Dancing is advancing, overall. When this forward movement is inevitable, it is convincing. This rule is a fundamental base for convincing and meaningful dancing.

Beginning in a dancing posture,[8] the arms moving forward (lifting from *bras bas* forward to any position) brings their combined weight forward. A typical adult arm is slightly less than 5% of the body weight, so the combined weight of both arms is about 9%. This weight displacement is not enough to cause the body to fall, but it does cause it to begin to move forward. As the body moves forward and the arms open, then the forward movement is balanced by the shift of weight from front to the sides (effectively from front back to the center of the body mass balance point). But, this arm movement has caused the body to arrive in this new location.

At the same time as the arms are causing the body to move forward and their opening is establishing a new balance point, there is also the sense of presenting one's self. It is a gesture of opening, presenting and being present for what is in front of the dancer. What has then been achieved is a quite convincing, inevitable and authentic movement. And as it finishes with an expression of openness of the upper body, it appears to be coming from within, from the heart.

Beyond the dramatic sense of this, there is a logic as well. The result is inevitable movement, but also intentional movement. There is nothing hesitant or withdrawn from this movement. It is certain, clear and quietly strong.

Every time the arms lift front and then open to the sides, a natural impetus for forward movement has occurred. Mechanically, to use the weight of the arms to initiate forward movement is an example of maximum effect with minimum force. It is efficient.

---

8 The dancing posture is achieved by a forward tilt of 4.5° of the center axis of the body. It places the top of the head above the center balancing point of the arches of the feet, and presumes that there is no break at the hip or ribs in the line of the body.

RETIRÉ IN BALLET MEANS 'PULL AGAIN'

The French terms of ballet as descriptions of both movement and purpose. As a ballet dancer is it very helpful to understand the actual meaning of the French terms used, and also their colloquial meanings within the ballet world. Too often the actual meaning, its intention and what it is describing, is lost and/or misinterpreted.

Here the term *retiré* refers to two different things at the same time. The adjective means "remote, out of the way". It describes the quality of the movement, and has a sense of urgency about it, like touching something hot and pulling your hand back quickly to get it remote from the heat and out of its way. In this sense, it would refer to any movement of a body part that takes it away from a place, or puts it out of the way. This is such as lifting one leg quickly into *passé*. This association of the term has remained in active use in ballet in the 21st century.

An older meaning is as a verb which means "pull again". This presumes that something had been pulled then relaxed and is pulled again. Specifically, it refers to the leg or legs being pulled to their full length in supporting the body, relaxing (into *demi-pliè*) and then returning to the fully "pulled" position. And so, when an exercise includes *demi-pliè, retiré* it refers to pulling the legs straight.

RULES OF ARRIVAL

In all dance forms, the movement IS the music. A dancer must be the music visually, and within that call is the fact that the body or part of the body (arm, leg, head, etc.) creates a visual accent the moment it arrives in a position or movement. This is the first consideration in dancing, for Rule #1 states "The Music Is Never Wrong."

Also, to properly create the mechanics of a movement different alignments and body shapes must be arrived at in a precise order, and with exact timing. If the body part has not arrived in time, or at the right speed, then the mechanics of that movement will be upset and result in incorrect placement, unsuccessful balance, bad timing and much more.

The Rules of Arrival are critical for ballet to achieve technical proficiency, and in order that the dancer is empowered to use artistry to the maximum of their ability.

Artistry begins with technical proficiency, refinement and the dancer's ability to have absolute control over the entire body at all times. Each movement is a choice, or should be. To lack control and therefore be unable to arrive, in part or in whole, at the precisely right time results in "chance dance", the state in which the dancer can only hope to balance, execute a number of turns or beats, to land in the right or intended spot, and all of the rest.

This sub section is critical for dancers to achieve ever higher levels within their career. Should these rules not be incorporated into the dancer's reliable tool kit, they will still dance, and dance well. But their dancing will never rise to the highest levels.

ACHIEVE FULL POSITION THE MOMENT THE FOOT TOUCHES THE GROUND.

With this rule it is important to know the meanings of French terms. The word *piquet* means "prick, poke, or sting" and refers to stepping onto a fully stretched leg, including the foot. The word *jeté* means "to throw". So by combining them, it means the dancer is arriving on a single stretched leg (ball of the foot or toe on the ground) having thrown the body's weight from the other leg. It is a very common movement, and can be done in any position, with or without turn.

The movement of a *piquet-jeté* is clear, and complete. The arrival is intact and denotes no further movement, though it often is followed immediately by other movements. And it is a quite common way to do a turn. All of this means that the moment of arrival atop the foot of the new standing leg is complete, the body whole. And likely it means balancing or turning in this position. Therefore, the whole body must arrive in its final position at the moment the toe touches the ground.

Perfecting this technique allows the dancer to place the entire body on an exact note of music, in a precise location, and achieve instant balance. To arrive in pieces (foot, hip, torso, arm, other leg in sequence for example) takes away expressiveness, directness and cleanliness, and makes musicality impossible.

Do not forget that the body is thrown from one foot to the other. And so the arrival position atop the new standing leg must be the apex of an arc. It is majestic, and confident. It is also triumphant. Soft or loud, shy or bold, surprised or surprising, it always catches the body arc at its apex and stays there.

Such certainty in the hands of a dancer allows them to make artistic choices. It gives control of expression and musical phrasing to the dancer, so that they can present to the viewer their interpretation of an authentic expression. This is the refinement of artistry.

ARRIVE IN FULL POSITION AT BOTTOM OF THE DEMI-PLIÉ.

This rule is simple. *Relevé* means "go up again" which assumes that the position you are in is the same and the action is merely to lift that entire position upward. But here is a commonly misunderstood part, for the only way to go directly upward is to spring up onto the foot bringing the ball of the foot (or point of the pointe shoe) to where the center of the arch of the foot had been. If one were to rise, then the weight transfers from that mid-arch forward to the ball of the foot, or even further forward onto the toe in full pointe.

Why talk about how to execute the mechanics of *relevé*? Because those mechanics define the rule quite specifically. There are many approaches to a *relevé*: *tombé*, *chassé*, *demi-pliè*, *jeté*, or spring down to *demi-pliè*. Only two of them (*demi-pliè* and spring down to *demi-pliè*) would have the body in the same position prior to the *relevé* as at the top of the *relevé*. The others (*tombé*, *chassé*, and *jeté*) have the body in a very different position before the *relevé* to after. Hence the rule.

As the definition of the action dictates that the body position be fully established in the *demi-pliè* before the *relevé*, applying this rule is more about what happens when arriving in *demi-pliè*. And it means that the instant the heel arrives at the base of the *pliè* the full body position is established.

This places the body in a balance in that position, essential for continuing. And if the *demi-pliè* is done properly, it means that at the base of the *pliè* the body is lifted, particularly the supporting hip, which requires a very fast movement of the entire body.

Consequently, due to the speed of arrival, there will be a *grand battement* effect from the lifted leg and possibly also the arms, that create an additional force of lift. And when the timing is done correctly, and the body rebounds from the base then the Ballet Magic rule comes into effect creating a dynamic and brilliant movement. If the dancer fails to lift their supporting hip, collapses the upper body or arms, or sits in the *pliè*, then the momentum is lost and the result is either a lumbering struggle to the top or the use of unnecessary tension and force to achieve something that should be quite light and easy.

FINAL LEG POSITION ACHIEVED BEFORE THE APEX.

When jumping in the air the body travels in an arc, even when the arc is purely vertical. The apex of that arc is the point of statement or expression of that choreographic element, for it is at the precise moment that the body shifts from traveling upward to returning to gravity producing an instant of stillness. In these moments, when done correctly, the body appears to be floating in the air (called 'hangtime'). This is spectacular to watch, but is not the reason the choreography has been created.

The reason for the jump is the arc the jump makes on its trajectory, and the end point position the arc leads to. The choreographer has created an elevated line for the viewer to see and follow as s/he make a living visual painting in space. Regardless the step, the final position of the body must be achieved in the air before the apex, which means the body arrives in its position and then that position continues to ascend to the apex. The dancer gets the moment of personal glory to have created a spectacular hangtime photo op, and the trajectory arc of that movement is also seen.

There are five categories of steps that fall under this rule. Below each is briefly described.

ASSEMBLÉ

In an *assemblé*, the leading leg uses *grand battement* effect simultaneously with the *frappé* push of the supporting leg on take off to lift the body upwards. Immediately, as soon as the body is airborne, the final assembled position of the body is achieved before the apex and while the body is still ascending.

JETÉ

In a *jeté* the same mechanics are applied to take off as in an *assemblé* so that the leg position (typically *coupé en arrière*, though there are limitless variants) is achieved once in the air but before the apex. This allows the eye to follow the whole body as it travels its trajectory, and gives time for arm movements to embellish that arc.

83

Basque steps are derived from the dances of the Pyrenees Mountain region in Spain where the Basque people originate from. Basque dancing is among the most complex in the world, and it combines an intricate and sophisticated system of rhythm, body attitude, and arm movements into an active and energized harmony.

Pas de Basque presents this harmonic flow on the ground and can be accented at any point.

Tour de Basque is a pointe step but can be done without pointe shoes. Leading with the advancing leg in front, the dancer springs *à côté* into 5th position en face having changed legs, then descends into *demi-pliè en tournant* that finishes a quick *soutenu renversé*. This is an extremely fast step that is brilliant. But the rule is that both feet must arrive in 5th position immediately.

Saut de Basque is a large air turn based on the element of the Basque dances in which one movement grows out of the preceding one. In this there are two arrivals, first *à la second en tournant en dedans* leaving the ground, followed by *grand battement passé en tournant en dehors* that lifts the body higher still. And so there are two arrivals, each at the start of ascension and before that apex.

BATTERIE

In all beats, the legs immediately beat when the body leaves the ground and continue beating to the apex and beyond, depending on how many beats are called for.

TOURS EN L'AIR

With *tours en l'air* the moment the body is off of the ground the arms and legs arrive at the final position, well before the apex. This initiates the spin, which continues to the apex and beyond, depending on the rhythmic intent. There is a variant in which the dancer jumps up to the apex and then changes the arms to turn on the way down, but this reads as heavy and forced, which may be a character choice depending on the choreography and the narrative.

REAR FOOT PASSES THROUGH FRONT LEG

It is important to avoid giving muscles the wrong directive with your thoughts and approach. Often thoughts of literal logic cause the wrong thing to happen. And with this rule there is a prime example.

When beginning in 5th position, given that the dancing posture is lifting up and forward at a slight tilt, more weight is on the front food, just slightly. And when the step calls for the legs to reverse positions (*changement, batterie*, lifting to *coupé devant*, etc.) it is important to direct the rear foot to go through the front leg to get to the other side of it. This causes the body to put the rear foot in front in the most efficient path.

Should the actual route from rear to front be in the mind, then the body gets the instruction to "go around the front foot to the front" and it will automatically use the quadriceps to open the leg as it goes around, which slows the movement, and displaces the balance of the body from its pure center line.

In the case of placing the leg from rear 5th to the *sur le cou de pied* position, having it in mind to clear the heel, rather than going through the front leg, causes the body to again go around by either activating the quadricep (most disruptive), the hip flexors (lifting the leg and knee up and out), or the sartorius (more efficient but still disruptive to the flow). Each is wrong, very inefficient, and will cause the working leg to lift away from the standing leg and then be placed back on the ankle. When this happens the placement of the leg back on the ankle becomes a downward movement both in weight displacement and the visual optics of it. And if the foot comes back to the standing leg and still is following the upward direction, then it lands too high to be a sur le cou de pied position and becomes *coupé côté*, which is an entirely different alignment of weight.

By applying this rule, the footwork is efficient, absolutely properly placed, and the overall trajectory of the movement beyond this instigating moment retains its intended expressive focus. It also keeps the mechanics of the body smooth and natural.

Rules of Ambulation

Often there is more focus on tricks and spectacular circus-like movements in ballet. Indeed crowds love this. But those easily achieved sensations are quickly forgotten, and make no expressive impact on the viewer. It makes the spectacle of ballet something to look at, rather than something to remember.

It is the ambulatory steps in ballet that tell the story, contain the dancing, and make a performance memorable. Simply, the ambulatory steps demonstrate the journey of the choreography, its purpose and intent. This is the human element between super human tricks. This is the body of the dancing.

There are specific rules about how one travels across the floor in dance, and different steps make different statements of expression. It is important to distinguish between the different steps and how they are to be done per these rules.

THE WEIGHT STAYS WITH THE LEADING FOOT.

Chassé is a smooth transition to a new location. From the very start of it, the weight stays with and on the leading foot, almost like a chug, but not so abrupt. During the movement the weight is neither on one nor the other foot, but is traveling with and in the direction of the leading foot.

The dancer must know precisely where, and in what body position, the arrival will be when it is complete. Sequential *chassés* are punctuated with a *sauté* in closed 5th position. With each new landing, the body weight is with the leading foot.

Should the weight rest on the back foot, it makes a lumbering gallop movement that is awkward and belabored. This step is to be smooth as silk, and eagerly and energetically forward moving. Delaying the weight transfer to the forward foot will result in a *tombé* movement, which is entirely different and does not have the sense of smooth kinetic flow.

Very important here is to determine where the body weight is at all times. And, of course, when arriving in each new position, the heel of the leading leg must be well forward so that the body is stable at all times, and there is no wiggle or involuntary adjustment to interrupt the clear statement of purpose the step is being used to convey in the choreography.

THE WEIGHT FALLS ONTO THE FOOT.

Tombé is about ambition, goal, certainty and achievement. These are the abstract qualities the movement conveys, regardless of the greater context of its use in a phrase. It also has an element of hesitation, uncertainty and the need for a plan in order to go forward.

The word *tombé* means 'fallen' as an adjective, or 'fall' as a verb. It has a downward thrust, and is earth bound, grounded. There is a static quality in this, like 'putting one's foot down' to make a point. The act of falling to a new position is not smooth, and is an outcome rather than a fluid intention. It can be done with a bounce to it, and is often used in folk dancing and national dance forms. It is a step of the people, the peasants, the farmers.

In this step, the weight of the body stays in the location of origin on the supporting leg, and then only falls onto the leading leg when the new location is achieved. There is no glide forward.

THE BODY REMAINS ON THE LEADING LEG THROUGHOUT.

The rule for *balancé* refers to the proper way to do the basic, academic step. This step takes its name from the act of balancing, and in this specific case it is about keeping the weight balanced over the leading foot, even as the following foot briefly tests that forward balance.

The rule allows the body to stay in one place, yet display rhythm. The brief step up on the non-leading leg is as if to demonstrate the balance on that leading leg. It is to be smooth and seamless, rather than bouncy and traveling back and front again.

As with all steps there are many ways to approach this, and indeed using a spring, lift, lilting rise, *petit jeté*, sustained movement and other varieties are all included among them. But the constant is that once the body weight arrives over the new location of the leading foot, there it stays regardless of the nature of the movement to the other leg and back.

This rule, having been consistently applied, makes the step appear as a single rhythmic element, rather than a bisected and irregular movement. In this way, attention is focused on the gesture, expression and meaning the movement has within the context of the choreography.

In terms of expression, sticking to this rule makes the step represent all of life's moments when there is something active happening (the rhythm within the step and found in the legs) yet the overall mood is the same. In a folk or national dance setting it is often the joy of dancing or the focus of competition between dancers that is the constant expression, with the rapid heart beat and demanding structure of the rhythm as the foundation. In grand waltz choreography, the implied swaying of a waltz underlays the sweeping and grand patterns of the dancing. A gentle or tender expression guides the beating heart of a lover, or a mother singing a lullaby to her child. And, as always in ballet, it can represent the hauteur of a Royal member who must maintain composure while the intrigues of the castle or unrest in the realm is going on beneath that regal surface.

THE WEIGHT IS BETWEEN THE LEGS, NEITHER ON ONE NOR THE OTHER

This is one of the most difficult rules for students to grasp, yet once grasped the sensation of it places it firmly in physical memory for the rest of their dancing. By the time a dancer is in their first years of study it is already automatic, because this rule applies to walking and running that is smooth and on a constant trajectory.

With this rule we find the zone between feet, the moment in which the weight remains between the feet even though the feet are hitting the ground as the body moves over them. It is the steady run, the smooth walk, the graceful gliding across a room.

Coming from the rule "Balance Toward the Working Leg", here we see the body just after balancing toward the working leg, when it has gone to a new working leg. But the body weight never comes to rest on either leg at all. It exists between the legs, never placing its weight on top of either leg.

There is a discrepancy in history about what this comes from, for Russian, Italian, French, Spanish and Portuguese cultures each have claimed its origin. In the Western European nations it is said to come from the wine industry, and specifically the workers who had to stomp the grapes. By keeping the body weight between the legs the workers did not tire so easily and could work for longer and more effectively. In Northeastern Russia, Siberia, there are many folk dance forms that come from needing to constantly be moving to keep the blood flowing and maintain the warmth of the body.

The *bourré* was thus borne in one form or another in all of those places. When it was incorporated into ballet there was a rivalry between the Czar of Russia and the King of France, cementing the prominence of this technique firmly in the cultures of both countries.

And it also applies to *enchaînement déboullés* (*Chainé* turns), *glissade* and other steps that glide smoothly across the floor.

RULES OF EFFECT

Ballet is properly called "Classical Theatrical Dancing", and as such it is all about expression and effect. The solid foundation of this fine art form of theater is found in the 284 distinct steps and movements that make up the lexicon of ballet movement. And within this system of human movement are systematic positions, body attitudes, and body lines.

In every fine art there is a fixed form that establishes conformity and a standard. Adhering to this standard is less than the minimum requirement, and identifies the work as belonging to that established art form. Beyond this identification through established standard is the fact that in every fine art form there is a high level of refinement.

With this system established in ballet, then the dancer and choreographer can produce powerful and/or subtle effects by slightly altering line, rhythm, dynamic and other elements. This section of rules covers these effects.

Movement cannot lie, and so when an effect is applied, it reads always with authenticity and integrity. When no effect is applied, the movement feels mechanical, flat and dull. And so the rules of effect are applied throughout one's dancing at all times.

In addition to these fixed rules of effect, a great number of the 100 rules of ballet impact effect as well. Moving the arms from the fingertips shows the effect of intent and inevitability; use of épaulement creates effect of internal impetus and investment; etc. All of these rules add to the depth and expressiveness of one's artistry as a dancer, and strengthen one's technical ability. They mark the difference between a dancer and a dance artist. Use them wisely.

GRAND BATTEMENT EFFECT APPLIES TO ANY BODY PART MOVING QUICKLY UPWARD.

Grand battement effect refers to a transfer of energy from an ascending limb is used to lift the torso where it connects. The faster the movement, the more momentum is created, causing the greatest force of lift applied to the pelvis (legs) or upper body (arms).

Grand battement effect in actual dance steps is always simultaneous at the point of impetus for a movement of the whole body, but can otherwise be added either sequentially or simultaneously to shape ongoing movement. Having this tool well at hand provides a possibility of artistic, musical and expressive shading. It is always available.

Classical choreography makes clever use of this. In some Bournonville passages a traveling jeté can be given a second lift to its arc by employing this rule in the arms just prior to the apex of the initial arc trajectory. In partnering, as well as in both male and female variations, grand battement effect is built into the choreography to accent musical passages and augment expression. Deft use of this tool is the mark of great artistry.

As will be explored in the Rules of Turning section of this book, *grand battement* effect is an essential part of pirouettes of all kinds. The quick upward motion of a *grand battement* instantly places the body in balance. Beyond this, then, because it is the *grand battement* force that lifts the pelvis and torso, it is then not necessary to push with the feet. This eliminates one of the greatest deterrents to successful pirouettes. For when the dancer pushes off of the floor two things happen. First they are pushing down which takes energy away from the lift, causing it to slow which disrupts a naturally balance. And when this push comes, it is not a push directly downward, but on an angle off of the center, which pushes the body weight to the opposite side, further disrupting balance. And these misalignments of balance happen at the moment of impetus, so that from the very start the only way to achieve balance is through tension or sitting heavily on the supporting hip, both of which inhibit turning.

All of this applies to jumps with batterie as well. Employing this rule is not only the mark of artistry, but also a fundamental tool for the mechanics of movements.

THE LINE OF THE BODY IS STRETCHED.

The effect known as *élongé* refers to a body line that is stretched, or made to look long. The rule of *élongé* refers to taking a recognized and established body line (*arabesque, attitude*, etc.) or a movement (*assemblé, jeté*, etc.) and stretch it long. This is done for effect, and the amount of stretch must never be so exaggerated that the original sense is lost.

This rule can be applied to any movement, line or body part. It is one of the many ways in which a dancer can make artistic decisions about how they will portray choreography. It is elective in performance, but when applied inappropriately can have a comedic or affected result that is undesirable.

This rule gives teachers, coaches, choreographers, directors, and critics a language to use. By telling a dancer that they are to perform a *tombé élongé* the dancer immediately understands what is required. It is also a way to distinguish between steps when discussing a dancing passage.

The rule can also be used in corrections. By telling a dancer that they are overdoing the *élongé* line on a landing, for example, and it is causing their back to collapse, it is very useful to the dancer.

Overall, the *élongé* rule creates the effect of yearning, expansiveness, grand generosity and more. These are artistic effects, lifting the overall artistic quality of dancing, and allowing the dancer to make artistic decisions.

THE BODY THRUSTS FORWARD.

The *élancé* effect is about trajectory arc, rather than body line. This effect is about lengthening the trajectory arc of a movement, making it reach further and be less high in its apex. The word '*élancé*' in French means 'slim', referring to something that is stretched thin. It is derived from the way a lance is thrown. Rather than arcing high in the sky, a lance is thrust forward, with slight arc lift but almost parallel to the ground. This movement is slim rather than plump.

The application of this rule of effect makes a strong and energetic statement. For example, in Act II *Giselle* there is a diagonal for Prince Albrecht that consists of *brisé élancé*. The effect is a robust effort on his part to fight back fate, escape the *Wilis* and remain alive. To do normal *brisé* misses the stark dramatic statement entirely.

Employing this effect is powerful and creates a continuity of movement that is unique. When applied to dramatic passages it becomes an explosive show of intent and passionate pursuit. In a repeated movement, such as in the example above, the body is in constant motion, parallel to the floor, and seemingly defying gravity due to its sheer power of force.

In comedic passages it can be a very funny attempt to extricate one's self from some presumed threat. Displaying such desperation to escape from something as innocuous as a kiss, or being assigned responsibility is hilarious. It gives the sense of a terrified jack rabbit, so skittish that it is running from something that is no threat at all, simply because of a jumpy or untrusting nature.

In a romantic passage, a lover propelling him/herself toward the object of affection, the effect is of unbridled passion and internal urges so strong as to defy gravity and speed. An impetuous lover, driven from the immutable power of the heart, is now clearly evident.

These are but a few examples of when one might apply this rule.

THE STRETCHED BODY LINE THRUSTS FORWARD.

The *éliogné* effect is a combination of both *élongé* and *élancé*. Here the stretched body line is also thrust forward long and low with a burst of focused energy. It denotes the effects of yearning and longing, with the impetuous and unstoppable need to traverse space and time in an impatient way. This is an ultimate effect that is powerful and speaks clearly to the public.

For an example, we turn again to Giselle, Act II. Here the ghost of Giselle and Prince Albrecht are crossing past each other in *grand assemblé éliogné à côté*. Each is trying desperately to unite from two sides of death, and fail to do so. Despite the impossibility of their desires, their repeated attempt is a poignant and tragic effort. The fact that the landing is a total collapse to the floor with the fingers actually brushing the floor, and then a sousous with arms in high 5th position accentuates the extremes and opposites at play, and shows that from exhaustion springs hope. A very powerful statement.

Éliogné is powerful and rare. Such a tool in the hands of a fine artist must be used sparingly and never arbitrarily. Artistry of expression depends on effect, and accomplished artists of ballet (both dancers and choreographers) know to use it only when needed to make a very extreme statement.

EXPRESSION IS ENTIRELY IN THE CLAVICLE JOINTS

There are 12 clavicle joints, 6 pairs. They are the joints where the fixed ribs join to the sternum. These 6 pairs in the front represent 10 pairs from those same ribs that connect to the spine in the back. This is because the lower two ribs have a single connection at the sternum, and then split as they travel around the sides and approach the spine. Their range of movement is subtle, and dancers must stretch these joints rigorously, as they constantly strengthen the muscles of the upper spine and back.

The way to achieve the maximum range of motion in the clavicle joints is found in the Body Mechanics[9] exercises. These exercises must be done every day on a continuous basis to keep the range of motion at its maximum and even increase that range.

In a normal proscenium theater setting, the facial expression will not be readable beyond the first 5 or so rows of seats in the orchestra area of the house. Yet, the slightest lift or incline of the clavicles reads as the expression of the dancer to the back of the largest auditorium. This is because the range of motion in this portion of the body is so limited, and takes such focus and strength to achieve, others know intuitively that such a result is due to strong emotion, deep intent and an inability to contain one's self.

By using the flexibility of these sets of clavicle joints, the head and arms will be caused to move a much greater amount. And when the incline, lift, tilt or retreat of the upper body is caused by these joints, then the frame of the arms and the line of the head can remain intact, preserving the classical harmony of line while displaying maximum expressiveness.

The final point is that this use of body movement literally stems from where the heart is in the body. Consequently, all movements of expression created in this way have a sense of authenticity that cannot be anything other than heart-felt emotion by the dancer (character being played).

---

9 "Academy Method: Body Mechanics" by Ken Ludden is one of the textbooks published by Fonteyn Academy Press. ISBN: 9781312587410; Lulu Publishing, October 9, 2014

SECTION 7 - RULES OF TURNING

As is said often, and has been written by every authoritative author about classical theatrical dancing, turning is an entire study in and of itself. So vital is it to choreographic expression, and so fundamental to the movement lexicon of ballet, that there are more rules governing turning than any other single aspect of ballet study. In fact, there are 23 rules.

As these rules are studied, it is imperative to actually learn them by doing them, not just as an intellectual exercise. While this is true of every rule having to do with human movement, it is even more critical with turning rules. Some rules, once understood, are easy to apply. With turning, the coordination is very complex. So complex, in fact, that the human mind cannot possibly grasp everything at once, other then through an overall sensation. And the only way to have the sensation is to feel it.

Early attempts are sometimes more successful than later attempts, which is ironic. But when a dancer tries something for the first time the body is free of assumptions and memories, so is able to work more holistically. Once some attempts have been made, then the mind has data to apply, which makes things fall out of coordination, and upsets the body's natural priority system, as well as its somatic sense.

There are four forces that cause turning: outside force applied, winding up and releasing energy to cause torque, transferred momentum, and internal turning (the "middle molecule" or "M&M"). This makes the world of turns far more complex, and therefore different rules will apply to different types of torque force incorporated into the turning recipe.

The first rules are the ones that apply to all turns, regardless of torque force origin. It cannot be emphasized strongly enough the importance of practicing each of these rules over and over, every day. Until these first basic rules of turning are ingrained into your body memory as automatic reflex actions, turns will be uneven, unpredictable and not within the control of the dancer.

Beyond this question of automatic and reliable mechanical responses in the body, is the question of rhythm, and internal rhythm of turns. These are the tools when used that lift the ability to turn from technical reliability to masterful artistry. Always aim higher.

TURN THE MIDDLE MOLECULE.

The absolute center of body mass is found in a single molecule. It is located (depending on exact proportions) in the center/center of the pelvis. This center-most point of body mass is the effective primogenitor of all turns, or the "very first ancestor" of a turn. Should the body be engaged, and this molecule turned, then the entire body will spin on its axis.

This idea is one of those that, while literally true, is a guide for the mind. When a dancer instructs the mind to turn this middle molecule, then a complex and body-wide coordination happens that causes the entire body to turn. And turning this molecule is able to produce enough torque force to turn the body 3 times, or a triple turn. Indeed, Academy students must do a triple turn in this way before being allowed to use 4th position in turn preparations.

The exercise itself—"Preparation for Pirouette"—is described in various Academy Method publications, and is part of both Level 1 and Level 2 curricula in the Lower School. It is worked into many *barre* exercises in all of Academy Method training, and employed regularly as a center floor exercise throughout all Academy Method training in both the Lower and Upper Schools.

This principle is the primary principle for all turns, for if the center mass of the body is not already turning of its own energetic force, then turns will not be achieved without tension in the body, excessive and unnecessary external forces being applied, and a perpetual and unpredictable struggle to determine the moment of turning and the number of revolutions to be achieved.

EVERY FIRST TURN BEGINS WITH THE HEAD.

Given that the middle molecule is in effect, the second rule of turning is that in any sequence of turns (including a sequence of one turn) the head leads the initial turn. By the sharp turn of the head being applied simultaneously with the lift of the pelvis via *grand battement* effect, and the elevation on the foot, the forces of lift and torque are united. The result is ease of turn, and control of every aspect of the turn by the dancer.

If the sequence of turns is for a double or more rotations on the axis, then "spotting" comes into play to further propel the torque force, manage the precise rhythm of the set of turns, and control the speed of rotation. That spotting also helps prevent dizziness is auxiliary to its actual function in the mechanics of turning.

The use of the head to lead the turning of the body is quite natural, and is what is used whenever anyone chooses to turn. Imagine you are walking along and from behind you hear someone call your name. You first turn your head in the direction of the origin of the call and that causes the entire body to turn in that direction.

By employing this rule turns are natural, have an ease, and remain balanced.

THE BODY AUTOMATICALLY BALANCES WHEN IN A NEW POSITION IS TAKEN QUICKLY.

The nature of all things in the physical universe is to balance. Any event has a simultaneous opposite and equal event, thus allowing perpetual change and constant balance.

The body works somewhat in the same way. When a person takes a misstep, or slips, instantly as the body goes out of balance the arms, head and other leg fly into a position to counter balance the falling body. This is instinctive, instantaneous and happens without thought. And in turns, the dancer can rely on this truth of the body.

When a sudden and new body position occurs, the body will instantly balance that new position. In turns, this is essential. Using a *grand battement passé* movement of the working leg to lift the pelvis upward in a normal *pirouette* will create an instantly balanced position. This assumes the body is functioning as an engaged whole.

Adding simultaneous arm movements can augment the force, speed and number of rotations in a turn, provided the body is in a position of balance. And the working leg must follow this rule with any position used in a turn, not only normal *pirouette*.

Should the dancer slowly lift the leg into position, or delay its arrival by first using it to push the body into turning and then lift to position, the body receives confused intention and balance will be helter-skelter, attempting a rebalance at each new position of the leg.

This also applies to shifting shape of the torso (sticking the ribs out, arching the lower spine, misaligning the shoulders, etc.) and sudden arm movements. Even the tilt and angle of the head will, if it changes or wobbles, change the balance of the body. Any such change mid-turn will upset the turn.

The only movement of the body that will not upset the balance of the turn is lifting or lowering the heel of the working leg during a turn (obviously not related to *pointe* work). To move from quarter-pointe to half-pointe will increase or decrease the speed of rotation (lifting up creates centripetal torque increasing the speed of rotation; lowering the heel produces centrifugal torque force that will slow the speed of rotation). But this lift does not alter the balance of the body position at all of its own influence.

THE WORKING LEG IS IN FULL POSITION AT THE START OF THE TURN.

This rule reiterates other rules of turning, but from a different perspective. The different perspectives are useful as corrections, for different dancers respond to different ideas.

The rule itself is simple. At the very start of the turn the working leg must be fully in place at the instant the turn starts. This means that it arrives as the head turns to commence the rotation. This establishes the balance, provides maximum *grand battement* effect force of lift, and establishes both line and starting body shape.

In some turns the leg position changes as the turn is in progress. Such turns do not negate this rule. Even when the shape and line of the leg will change during the turn, at the instant the turn begins, the working leg must be in the full starting position of the turn.

PIROUETTES USE DYNAMIC BALANCE.

A *pirouette* is a step, and as such it comes before and after other steps. A smooth transition between steps is always part of dancing, as well as the ability to end a step on the spot. The ability to do this in a pirouette calls for the dancer to be in a balance throughout the turn that is dynamic—i.e., that can go from there to any other position or stop in place.

This means that the actual balancing position in a pirouette is not a static balance, but is a fluid balance. Where a static balance is the result of tension, or sitting heavily on the supporting hip, a dynamic balance is achieved by being directly at the pinnacle of the vertical axis of the leg.

This relates back to the rule "balance toward the working leg" as the purely vertical length of the leg is found only in 1st position, where the center of the hip is atop the center of the straight leg. To take a balance from 5th or 3rd position means the leg will be at an angle. Not only is this lower to the ground, it also causes the body weight to sit heavily on the angled leg, In a turn, this means that the force of the turn will be pulling the body weight because it is off center to the turning axis of the balance of the body.

It is difficult for may dancers to understand the dynamic balance until the gluteus medias is strong enough to maintain a balance on top of the leg, with the hips level, and the supporting leg centered in the hip socket, rather than the center of the torso. This position is impossible until the outer muscles of legs and hips are strong enough to maintain it. But once this strength has been achieved, this rule can then be fully utilized.

TURNING IS FALLING.

This rule seems contradictory to logic. Once the full ability of the body is taken into account, and all of the muscles trained and strengthened, it begins to make sense. This rule requires the dancer achieve a Balance, suspended in a very slow fall, on a completely vertical leg.

Again, as with Rule #81, this allows the dancer to blend the step before the turn into the turn, and then allows the dancer to flow fluidly from the turn into the next position.[10] When a turn is viewed as an arc of movement, rather than a static position that turns in place, the timing of the suspension at the top is in transit rather than in a fixed position. This allows in an extreme amount of lift, and light and airy sense, and a brilliance of rhythm which give artistry to the turn.

This rule also relates to the rule that calls for a balance toward the working leg. When the dancer is suspended on a fully vertical leg, knowing that this suspension is leading to a fall from that place, it gives the dancer the ability to control this very slow rate of fall so that musicality and timing are part of their artistry.

Once the dancer surpasses 5 revolutions in a turn the form of the turn changes, and indeed a turn may be settled into, for with extreme multiple turns the focus is on the repeated internal rhythm rather than the turn and its rhythmic presence being treated as an elemental step within a larger phrase.

It is rare that choreography calls for more than a quadruple turn, so this special case exists external to this rule for turning. In fact, it is rare that choreography calls for more than a triple turn in classical dancing.

By embracing the rule that turning is falling, it opens up a completely new approach to how one might use a turn within the larger phrase. Is it a high point? Is it the catalyst that propels a forward motion that otherwise would not exist or is unexpected? Is it simply an embellishment to a larger, more cohesive phrase?

And also a result of artistic use of this rule is the vast array of expressions turns can become. All of this is a result of this rule.

---

10 Remember that a turn finishes on top of the working leg. Coming down from a turn is the beginning of the next step.

TURN THE ENTIRE BODY.

The final general rule for turning is one that is often foreign to even accomplished dancers. As logical as it seems, the truth of it is often forgotten. So much emphasis is placed on balancing in turns that it is quite typical for a dancer to place their body into a static balanced position and then box their way around to cause that position to turn on its axis.

In fact, as a dancer travels from preparatory position to the turning position, the body is already in rotation. If, for example, the arms in a turn are to go to high 5th position from a normal pirouette preparatory arm position, the arms do not lift directly upward as though the body will remain facing the point of origin. Instead, by the time the arms reach their apex, the body will already have turned 180-270°.

As a dancer learns to work with this rule, they must lift from preparatory arm position to final arm position in an upward spiraling rotation. The same is true for the shoulders, hips, and entire body. Therefore the rule "turn the entire body".

In a turn such as repeated *tours à la seconde*, where the arms remain in a fixed position in relationship to the torso, the fingertips must be traveling up and down in a circular motion centered on the body's central axis, so that the entire body is constantly turning.

By reminding a dancer to turn the non-working side of the body, or bring around the shoulder blade of the back, it causes the body to turn as a whole, so there is no drag or sluggishness on the force of turn.

ARMS AND TURNS

One arm is approximately 4.5° of the body's weight, and both together represent approximately 9° of the body's weight. Singly or together, the arms can greatly impact the trajectory and balance of the body. Arms are also extremely mobile, as well as articulated at shoulder, elbow and wrist, so that the precise placement and shape is instrumental in shaping movement.

With turns, since arms have a year 360° rotational capacity (this being expandable through stretches and exercises for the arm and shoulder), they can be used as a creator of momentum, a balancing agent, a dispeller of momentum, or a catalyst for another part of the body to move.

The four rules for arms in relation to turns provide the guidelines for the classical use of arms. This does not mean the classical position of arms, nor does it mean the established system of *ports des bras* each method of dancing includes in its basic forms. It refers to the classic ways in which, categorically, the arms are used with and for turns.

BALANCE THE MOVEMENT, NOT THE POSITION.

Arms are completely dynamic. They can change shape and position in many, many ways. They can create balance and imbalance. They can create or dispel momentum. They are living, moving, shape-shifting elements of the body. When a body takes a position, even though a specific arm position is usually part of the design, they can adapt to the specifics of the individual body, its unique distribution of weight and mass. The only problem is that this approach balances the position, and should anything happen to radically change the position, the arms are not necessarily capable of correcting the balance.

But in a turn, the arms must balance the movement rather than the position. There are many forces of movement that balance the physical body. Think of a top, quite large at its equator, flat and broad at the top, and a tiny point at the bottom to balance on. When spinning, it balances perfectly yet the shape of it is nearly impossible to balance when still.

A turning body is the same. Nearly any physical position , so long as there is a basic centering or symmetry of the shape, will balance when spinning, while when still will not balance. The effect can be spellbinding for the viewer, and even magical. When in a turn, the arms must balance the movement of the turn. When used in this way, choreographers can be extremely creative, and the range of expression becomes vast.

As a dancer, it is important to feel the movement, and find the kinetic, dynamic balance of that movement. The urge of some dancers to find a position that balances when still and then turn it becomes an obstinate predilection. This mind set is useless to creative choreographers. The result of this approach places a bland look to choreography, as if the dancer can only turn in one position, or a fixed and limited set of positions. It can make inventive and expressive choreography seem inconsequential, and even boring.

Dance is meant to be alive, to express the living human situation. By feeling the entirety of the turn, and finding the kinetic balance with the arms, allows for brilliant expressiveness, inventive choreography and a far greater range of movement language.

RULE 85: PREPARATION RULE

THE PREPARATION IS THE TURN.

In pottery there is a saying: "The pot is in the throw." This refers to the use of a potter's wheel, which is a motorized spinning disk of stone onto which a lump of moist but solid clay is thrown. The moment the clay hits the wheel and begins to spin the potter starts shaping the clay into the pot they will make. If the lump of clay lands directly in the center of the wheel, then the sides of the entire pot will be uniform thickness, and there will be no wobble as it spins to create irregularity in the result. So the more perfect the throw, the more perfect the pot.

The preparation rule is derived from the potter's rule directly. For the more perfect the preparation for the turn, the better the turn will be. And here there are several considerations. The first is identical to the centeredness of the clay on the wheel. In a turn from 3rd, 4th or 5th position, the weight of the body must be exactly centered over the foot of the supporting leg in the turn.

Since the majority of *pirouettes* are done from 4th position, this means that the center of the body weight must fall directly over the front foot—and remain there. This centering on the front foot happens at the base of the *demi-plié* in such a way that the rear foot is touching the floor, but it bears no weight. From this position it is then quite easy to lift the knee upward and heel forward in the *grand battement passé* that will lift the hips upward for the turn, and establish the balance and position for the turn.

Yet this rule is for all *pirouettes*, not just those from 4th. Turns can come from any position at all, and the mechanics of unusual turns must be worked out by the dancer so that the preparation serves the turn. Various categories of *pirouettes* from two feet are covered in this section of Turning Rules. But this rule also covers arms, head, shoulders, pelvis and every other part of the body.

Make an active practice to study all of the many types of turns, and study them in relation to the preparations used for each. The more practiced the dancer is with this rule, the better an overall turner the dancer will become.

Often a preparation is quite well done, but between the preparation and the turn the dancer will shift the weight, do a second, deeper *demi-plié*, change the arms, or many other things between the preparation and the actual turn. Whatever the movement/position that directly precedes the turn is the preparation, and this is what is meant by this rule.

THE ARMS ARRIVE AT THE START OF A PIROUETTE.

Related to the rule that the body will balance whatever position it arrives in quickly and simultaneously, this specifically speaks of the arms. From the preparation position, the arms must instantaneously move to their turning position, along with the whole body, to establish the balance for the turn.

One must remember, though, that often the arms are one of the forces of turn (torque) that will create the spin of the turn by virtue of the route they take from preparation to turning position. This route, in accordance with this rule, must be completed by the time the body arrives in its turning position, making the movement of the arms very fast.

Should the arms move before or after the arrival; or be slowed so they start early or finish late (or both) then the turn will be lopsided and fail unless tension, or some other unwelcome element is employed to maintain balance.

The arms must be coordinated and even, for the relationship between motion and momentum is such that the faster a limb moves the more momentum it creates. Should one arm provide a different sort of momentum than the other, the turn is again upset, the torque is uneven, and it will fail unless an unwelcome element is used to save it.

If the arm movement is complex, or unusual, then it must be practiced repeatedly so that it is automatic. If the position of the arms in a turn is unusual, then that position and the movement from their position in the preparation to their position in the turn must be practiced until it is automatic.

And many turns incorporate arm movements during the turn. In this case, the movement of arms from preparation to starting position in the turn must be done so that they arrive in their designated position at the start of the turn, even if they then continue to perform some other movement to shape the turn itself.

Never forget that all arm movements are led by the fingertips, and all arm movements come from the impetus created by the upper torso.

The whole porte de bras occurs during the pirouette.

Choreographic expression in pirouettes often is achieved by arm movement while turning. The arms may begin in low 5th position as the turn begins, and then be lifted gradually ending in high 5th position at the end of the turn. There is a *pirouette* that employs *4me porte de bras* as the turn happens. The possibilities are limitless.

This rule states that the entire *porte de bras* must be executed in the same time as the turn takes to complete. If the arm movement begins before the turn starts, then its function in the mechanic of the turn is lost or out of sync. If a pirouette begins without the arms, and they catch up during it, again the function of the arms in the mechanic of the turn is lost. If the body turns and the arms are left behind (the result when they are not actively placed in their position) they create a counter-force that will impact the turn and balance. Similarly, if the arms continue to move after the body has stopped turning, then there is a precipitated force that will interfere with ending and placing the turn.

It is imperative that the full *porte de bras* begins with the turn begins, and finishes when the turn finishes. Not employing this rule leads to what is called "chance dance" due to the uncertainty of the exact result. However, employing this rule gives the dancer control over their turns, and therefore they can make and execute artistic decisions with precision and intention.

CATEGORIES OF PIROUETTES

There are many categories of *pirouettes*, and many types of turns. These basic types each has a rule associated with it, which will be included in this section.

The first four rules pertain to the four basic types of *pirouettes*: *tire bouchant, Adagio, allegro,* and *dégonflé.*. Contrary to common presumptions, the difference between these is not the speed of the turn itself, but rather the mechanism for arriving on the lifted heel for the turn, and the mechanism for returning the heel to the ground afterward. This differentiation results in three uniquely distinct qualities of movement in rotation.

TYPE	ASCENT	DESCENT
ADAGIO	*ÉLEVÉ*	PRESSURE DOWN
TIRE BOUCHANT[11]	*ÉLEVÉ*	SPRING DOWN
ALLEGRO	*RELEVÉ*	SPRING DOWN
DÉGONFLÉ	*RELEVÉ*	PRESSURE DOWN

FIGURE 1 - TABLE OF *PIROUETTE* TYPES

At issue in this distinction is the placement of the center of the body's mass atop the supporting leg. And depending on the route taken to the top of that leg, the actual trajectory of the body comes into play. For dancers and choreographers alike, active knowledge of these types of turns renders the resulting work far more nuanced, expressive and impactful. Since classical theatrical dancing is a performed fine art form, it is not merely a matter of dazzling the audience with multiple rotations. The shape, speed, mood and expression of a body in rotation are among the thousands of tools in the hands of dance artists. The more depth of understanding, and facility of technical ability, one has, the greater the resulting work of art for both creator and interpreter.

---

[11] This is the proper name for a normal *pirouette*.

PRESSURE UP; SPRING DOWN.

In a *tire bouchant pirouette*[12] the dancer elevates using pressure of the ball of the foot pushing down on the floor, and then springs down at the end centered without changing vertical axis on the way down. In short, *tire bouchant pirouettes* are done with pressure rise to lift up, and then springing down into *demi-plié* to finish. In French, *tire bouchant* means "cork screw." And like a cork screw, these most common of turns rotates as it pulls up, then pops out of the top to land. The entire aesthetic of the turn perfectly mimics the action of a cork screw.

By using pressure to elevate the body, the dancer is applying centripetal force in the rotation of the supporting heel as its radius shrinks. By continuing to lift, the actual turn increases in speed. This produces a quickening cadence of rotation and rhythmic spotting resulting in the rhythm of single, double, triple and quadruple turns. Beyond four rotations the dancer must fall into a regular rhythmic movement of the head (spotting) to keep the momentum of the turn going. In each of the multiple *pirouettes* mentioned, the final turn is the quickest, and serves as a finishing accent to the internal rhythm of the turn. When such a turn finishes, and then the dancer springs down returning the heel to the floor without a shift of central axis, it serves to brighten the kinetic sense of the turn. This allows the dancer a type of kinetic punctuation, if you will, to the rhythmic presentation of the expression embodied in the turn.

---

[12] *Tire bouchant pirouettes* are the most common ones, and in Academy Method, when a combination is given and it includes a "*pirouette*", this indicates a *tire bouchant pirouette* unless otherwise stated.

PRESSURE UP; PRESSURE DOWN.

An *adagio pirouette* occurs when the dancer uses pressure both to rise to the top of the supporting leg, and to descend at the finish of the turn. This use of centripetal force on elevation, but the necessity of extreme control to melt back down onto the earth, renders a deep, lush sense of the turn, regardless of the speed of the turn. *Adagio pirouettes* begin and end with the footprint on the floor being at the same spot, but during the turn, the central axis of the body travels toward the center of the turning platform on the floor, and therefore has a rounder, softer type of aesthetic to it.

Often *Adagio pirouettes* are indeed slower than the other types, but that is not why they are classified as *Adagio*. The classification comes from the fact that using pressure to go from preparation to top of turn and back is the slowest way to arrive on a turning axis, and being that this occurs on both ends of the turn, it is therefore called *Adagio*.

But *Adagio pirouettes* themselves can be extremely fast. An example of this is found in many forms of character choreography in classical theatrical dance. There are *pirouettes* in *demi-plié*, fast turns that begin and end with the ball of the working leg on the floor to the side, turns that start fully lifted and then gradually descend in *demi-plié* to end on one knee, etc. In many more contemporary works of concert dance there are elements of jazz, modern and urban dance that employ a wide variety of *Adagio* turns in quite innovative and expressive postures, and having them done as *Adagio pirouettes* gives the dancer more control to the speed of rotation, adjustment to changing body posture and evolution of expression in the movement.

Spring up; Spring down.

The *allegro pirouette* is the product of springing onto the top of the turning axis and then springing back down. In this type of turn, not only is the central axis of the dancer's body in a fixed vertical position, the turn itself becomes instantaneous in that the moment the dancer arrives he is turning.

By employing this rule, turns easily become single elements of music, seemingly coming from nowhere, and punctuating a musical moment with a dizzyingly fast turn. But again, as with *Adagio pirouettes*, the name does not derive from the speed of rotation of the turn, but from the fact that springing up and down from a vertical axis for turning is the very quickest way any turn position can be achieved.

Allegro pirouettes are able to be placed in very specific and fixed positions in the design of the stage, and can also be refined in such a specific way that groups of dancers can dance in unison with an absolute oneness of *esprit de corps*. These turns are also quite common in *coda* sections of classical works. They are fast, spectacular, and very exciting to watch.

SPRING UP; PRESSURE DOWN.

In a *pirouette dégonflé* the dancer springs onto the ball of the foot spinning as in a burst of energy that turns from within, but then the turn slows as the dancer descends with pressure. It is a type of *pirouette* first named in Academy Method, though it has been used in choreography and interpretation in many dramatic and modern works.

In the discussions to form Academy Method, Margot Fonteyn remarked that she had made the choice to execute some turns in this way because it suited the character and the feeling of the ballet. In particular she spoke of times in the choreography for Juliet that this way of doing *pirouettes* seemed much more like youth, to charge full force into something only to soon learn it was not the best choice, or that there were other things to consider. She called it impetuous then tamed, and sometimes she referred to it as moments of great determination that deflated when you are undone by that which comes next.

The naming of this type of *pirouette* indeed was prescient on Fonteyn's part, because it is used more and more in the 21st Century. Contemporary dancing has embraced this type of *pirouette* so frequently that it has become one of the identifying elements of contemporary work.

Indeed, this rule comes directly from Fonteyn, and is evidence of how deeply she considered technical application to illuminate and clarify the artistry possible for ballet. This rule by virtue of its existence illuminates the need for fine artistry in ballet in order to fully communicate with the public.

ARRIVE TURNING.

There has been an extreme amount of evolution in the technique of *piquet-jeté en tournant en dedans* (*piquet* turns). This rule establishes the pure form of this step in its original application and technique.

Taking into consideration the technique for *piquet-jeté* we know that it is when the body weight is thrown (*jeté*) from one foot to the other, arriving on a straight leg and extended foot (*piquet*), and when done properly the instant the leading toe touches the ground, the entire body is in its fully achieved position.

This rule pertains to this basic step being used as a category of turn (*en tournant*). It means that instead of arriving in a balance on the leading toe or ball of the foot, one arrives (balanced, of course) actively turning. And the application of this rule brightens the resulting turn to brilliance.

To incorporate this rule forces the dancer to plan, think, practice and time the turn with precision. When viewed, it is clear that there is intent and determination coming from within the dancer. It allows the dancer to place the turn in music, and increases the potential speed at which these turns can be done.

By arriving turning, it also makes possible the proper application of Rule 78 which stipulates that the head movement leads all turns. As this step has evolved the use of the head has been reversed, being left behind and then catching up as the dancer lands in *demi-pliè*. By using this rule, and arriving turning onto the leading leg, the resultant proper use of the head accentuates the purpose and intent of the dancer.

THE TURNING FOOT REPLACES THE LEADING FOOT - EXACTLY.

For *piquet-jeté en tournant en dehors* (Lame Duck turns), there is a rule making it a different category of turn from *en dedans*. With many aspects of ballet, simply changing direction creates and entirely new technique.

Here the preparation is a *demi-pliè* on the leading leg (usually the result of a *tombé* though it can also be the result of a *chassé*). This is very important, because where the foot is placed in the *demi-pliè* becomes the exact location of this turn, thanks to this rule.

Again, the name of this category of turn begins with *piquet-jeté* indicating that the body is thrown from one leg to the next, and the moment the arrival leg's toe hits the ground the entire body is in its full position. This means that the body is airborne between legs.

The rule is that the toe of the supporting leg in the turn lands exactly in the same spot as the leading foot in *demi-pliè*. And to be very clear here, the toe lands in the spot beneath the apex of that foot's arch, dead center, and EXACTLY where that foot was. Indeed, the body must be airborne in order to do that.

By employing this rule, the spin is crystal bright, and can be intentionally placed, with great precision, precisely where the dancer chooses. In addition, the presence of the turn in the music is also under control of the dancer.

It cannot be overemphasized that the application of these rules, all 100 of them, is the very substance of artistry. In this fine art form of classical theatrical dancing, the artist only rises to that distinction when these rules are applied with consistency and reliability. An interpretation of a role is far more than just doing the steps or something like them. And interpretation is not a diary entry of how the dancer is feeling that day. Interpretation is an entire series of artistic decisions of phrasing, musicality, rhythm, expression, character arc, intention, and abstract communication with highly refined body language. It is fine art, not chance dance.

BE IN THE FINAL POSITION AT THE BASE OF THE DEMI-PLIÈ.

In the category of *relevé* turns, the rule is distinctly different than in other turns. The fact that this is done with a *relevé* means that the ball of the supporting foot (or toe if *sur les pointes*) replaces the center of the same foot (the center point under the arch of that foot). This is done with a push from the heel so that the body leaves the ground just enough to fit the extended foot. And it is done so that the upward thrust of the body is captured precisely at the apex of that vertical arc without over jumping it and landing heavily on the top of the foot.

To do this, at the moment one arrives at the base of the *demi-pliè*, the whole body is in its full position for the turn. There is no climbing up into position, or gradual lift of the leg, arm, head or any other part of the body after arrival. Again, the entire body must be completely in its turning position at the base of the *demi-pliè*.

This means that the body will arrive quickly in that position, effectively creating *grand battement* effect to lift the body. This, when simultaneous with the *frappé* push to create lift as well, there is a clean sharpness to the movement.

It gives the impression that the turn comes from nowhere, just materializes as if by magic. And it reads as the absolute intention of the dancer. In addition, it achieves an instantaneous balance so there is nothing arbitrary or inadvertent happening. The dancer is absolutely in full control of the turn, and all of its various elements—artistry.

THE WEIGHT OF THE BODY LEADS.

In a *chassé relevé* turn, Rule 94 applies, but in addition, the body leads as the *chassé* travels to its intended destination. There is no lagging behind, nor is there any punctuated landing in a *demi-pliè* that accentuates this turn as there is in a *relevé* turn.

The application of this rule gives an additional momentum to the movement that can be used in whatever way the dancer chooses. This momentum comes from the forward movement of the body into the base of the *demi-pliè*. This momentum is then transferred to the center axis of the body giving an additional force of turn.

This rule is about power, both literal and symbolic. The result is the sense that there is absolute commitment to the movement, and also an authenticity. The dancer is swept up in a movement, or feeling, that makes the turn inevitable. Whether that feeling is joy, fear, ambition, fury, or any other compelling human emotion is up to the dancer to convey.

The mechanics of this step, with the rule applied, show evidence of forces far greater than any human being. Thus it opens the possibility that some unseen force is at play, creating powerful magic on the stage.

RULES FOR MULTIPLE TURNS

There is a constant quest for achieving multiple turns in dancers of every generation and from every dance tribe distinction. Spinning is beautiful to watch, fun to do, and joyous all around. But as a dancer, and an artist, every movement must be decided so that artistry is present.

And so there are rules for each number of revolutions in a turn. The rules vary. Some are about mechanics, others rhythm, preparation, technique or style. Each is specific to the number of revolutions in a turn.

In this section there are five rules, progressing from a single revolution in a turn up to 5 revolutions. The reason it stops at 5 is because the rule is the same for 5 or more.

Each progressive number of turns has its own technique—they are different turns. This indicates that simply going up onto one leg and spinning, seeing how many might be done, simply does not happen unless five or more turns is selected by the dancer.

Technical rules about turns based on number of revolutions present a dancer or dance student with a challenge. It means that there is a choice to make before the preparation to turn. The choice is to be based on artistic considerations, and once determined, whatever choice is made, the execution of that decision is completely under the control of the dancer.

SINGLE PIROUETTES—ANY POSITION, NO PREPARATION.

Lifting upward while turning the head and the middle molecule will turn the body in any position. A single pirouette needs nothing, can come from nowhere and is very simple. While there is a eurythmic cadence to a single turn, it does not have a complex internal rhythm.

This rule is more a reminder than an instruction. It emphasizes the fact that a single turn is achievable in any circumstance. Since it requires no preparation, and very little energetic force, there is almost no feeling associated with the turn itself. Certainly, there is no sensation of turning. And this confuses dancers who rely on the sensation of a turn to validate that they are in fact turning.

The reminder of this rule is two-fold. First, it indicates that turning is easy and simple, not a big deal at all. And secondly, it reminds dancers that it is unnecessary to do any elaborate or energetic movement to achieve a single turn. In fact, complex and energetic preparations and mechanics will ruin the turn and often tip the balance in a catastrophic way.

DOUBLE PIROUETTES HAVE THE RHYTHM OF A HEARTBEAT.

Any double beat in dance has the rhythm of a heartbeat, with emphasis on the second beat. This "lub-dub" rhythm lands heavily on the second beat, which also comes quicker than expected after the first. There is a sense of urgency brought by the second beat, that is lively and energized.

In double turns the rhythm is what makes it a double, instead of simply two rotations. Turning around twice before finishing a turn is not a double turn at all. It is only a double when it has that rhythm.

The subconscious rhythm of a heartbeat reads in a subliminal way to the viewer. It unites the dance with the human nature shared by all. There is something comforting about that rhythm because it is the very first rhythm we each experience while in utero. It unites us with the mother, and each time the heart beats, a surge of nutrients, blood, oxygen and more rushes into the fetus through the umbilical cord. All of this is subliminal, and will not rise to the level of conscious awareness unless there is a concerted effort to do so.

But that interconnectedness of all human beings lends authenticity and integrity to the movement for both dancer and viewer. A properly executed double turn is the most common turn done in dancing.

TRIPLE PIROUETTES USE A "CROSSED 4TH.

We now, with this rule, venture beyond the rhythmic sense of a heartbeat, though it is right there in the internal rhythm between the second and third revolution of the body. And to do this, it is now necessary to add torque from the 4th position of the preparation.

While it is possible to do a triple turn without preparation, this turn will likely lack the specific rhythm of a triple, and more likely simply achieve three revolutions on the vertical axis. And this is where the preparatory position is used to make the turn a true triple.

The crossed 4th position of the legs is used, meaning that the 4th position is derived from the 3rd position alignment of feet and legs (as opposed to a 4th position that is derived from 1st position, and without the more extreme crossing of the legs in a 4th position that is derived from 5th position.)

The position of the feet, opened from 3rd position to 4th, places a slight tension in both hip joints. Because the full weight of the body is over the front leg (the same leg as the supporting leg in the turn), it places a bit more tension on the back hip than the front. And this slight residual tension in the hip will, when that rear leg uses *grand battement* force as it lifts to *passé*, elevating the pelvis and establishing the balance position. This residual force added to the normal force of a double is more than adequate to cause the triple turn to occur.

QUADRUPLE PIROUETTES USE A FULLY CROSSED 4TH POSITION, AND WITH STANDARD PIROUETTE ARMS.

A quadruple *pirouette* comes from a fully crossed 4th position—one derived from 5th position. The residual torque force in the hip of the lifting leg is far greater than the 4th used for triple pirouettes.

Also in a quadruple *pirouette*, the standard preparatory arms (both classic and neo-classic stylization) are now used. They are unified in effort, and applied simultaneously with the head turn, grand battement passé, downward push with the supporting leg, and lifting from the top of the head with kneecaps arriving first. This simultaneous and unified motion creates a great deal of torque force.

As with a triple *pirouette*, the quadruple's final two rotations retain the internal rhythm of a double with two even rotations before it. Again, simply spinning in four consecutive rotations is not considered a quadruple *pirouette*, but just spinning four times before landing. The distinction is very evident to those watching, and ads an exciting element of expression.

MULTIPLE PIROUETTES USE AN "OPEN 2ND POSITION" AND ARMS MOVE SEQUENTIALLY.

When there are 5 or more rotations in a pirouette the entire mechanic and nature of the turn changes. The internal rhythm of each rotation is identical, and the dancer can elect to finish the turn any way at all.

The internal rhythm of each turn is expressed by the grouped syllables "dig-id-a; dig-id-a; dig-id-a…". These turns are evenly spaced across time. The speed of the spotting head can increase or decrease the rate of rotation at will. The dancer can also lift the heel higher to speed up the rate of rotation, or lower it as far as quarter point to slow it.

The preparation position is called "open 2nd" position. It is achieved by starting in 2nd position and moving the working hip and leg slightly back from the center line, while at the same time moving the shoulder blade, arm and shoulder the same amount forward of the center line, as if a mirror. The tension between the two is felt, and when released at the moment of *grand battement passé*, spins the body quickly.

At the same time, the leading arm opens to second position, and the trailing arm then overtakes it and rides on top of it crossed at the hands, so that fingertips of each hand aligns with the wrist of the other hand. However, the open 2nd position of the arms occurs at the moment of 180° rotation, and the hands overtake and cross (trailing hand above leading hand) at the 360° rotation point.

And all of this—head, leg, hip, shoulder, arms and hands—happen simultaneously. This causes enough torque to sustain five or more rotations, and the subsequent action of the head and lift of the heel can increase and decrease the speed of rotation at will.

www.ingramcontent.com/pod-product-compliance
Lightning Source LLC
Chambersburg PA
CBHW022004170526
45157CB00003B/1138